Partnerships of Hope:

Building Waldorf School Communities

Partnerships of Hope:

Building Waldorf School Communities

by

Christopher Schaefer

Printed with support from the Waldorf Curriculum Fund

Published by:
Waldorf Publications
38 Main Street
Chatham, New York 12037

Title: *Parnerships of Hope:*
    Building Waldorf School Communities
Author: Christopher Schaefer
Editor: David Mitchell
Copy Editor and Proofreader: Ann Erwin
Cover: David Mitchell
© 2012 by Waldorf Publications
Reprinted 2013
ISBN # 978-1-936367-20-7

Printed by McNaughton & Gunn
Saline, MI 48176 USA

Table of Contents

Hope

Either we have hope in us or we don't. It is a dimension of the soul, and it's not essentially dependent on some particular observation of the world or estimate of the situation. Hope is not prognostication. It is an orientation of the Spirit, an orientation of the heart. …

Hope, in this deep and powerful sense, is not the same as joy that things are going well, or willingness to invest in enterprises that are obviously headed for early success, but rather an ability to work for something because it's good, not just because it stands a chance to succeed.

Hope is definitely not the same thing as optimism. It is not the conviction that something will turn out well, but the certainty that something makes sense, regardless of how it turns out. …It is also hope, above all, which gives us the strength to live and continually try new things, even in conditions that seem hopeless.

– Vaclav Havel (1986)

Dedication

This book of essays is dedicated to my children, Karin and Stefan, and to their children, Kaya, Cyris, and Talei, in the hope that they will experience a world of increased educational freedom and creativity, an education dedicated to service and to peace.

Preface

It was a cold day in early March when I went to pick up my grandson at the kindergarten of the Brooklyn Waldorf School. As I walked down Hanson Street, the wind was blowing hard as it often does on streets with tall office buildings. When I pulled the door open at the school building next to the Brooklyn Academy of Music, I could hear singing and laughter as well as children's chatter and the lower modulated voices of parents. There were smiles, greetings and hugs as we waited on the stairs and in the hallway for the doors of the cramped classroom to open. Then the children appeared under thick hats and coats, smiling as they saw the faces of parents and grandparents. After a quick greeting we trudged hand in hand down the long stairs, the children waving goodbye to their friends and classmates.

In remembering this day and the children's celebration of the Chinese New Year festival I had experienced a few weeks previously, I reflected on my many years of deep connection to the Waldorf School Movement: first as a student, then as a founding parent at a new school and also as an active parent in three other Waldorf schools, and later as an advisor to many Waldorf schools in the United States and abroad. I also remembered the many years as a faculty member at Sunbridge College and our efforts to build programs serving the needs of the Waldorf movement and of anthroposophy. A feeling of gratitude came to me as I pondered this life-long connection to Waldorf education and my involvement in the efforts to build vibrant, joyful and life-enhancing Waldorf school communities.

This book of essays is written out of this experience with Waldorf education. It is for the children, teachers, parents, administrators and friends of this unique educational movement that is worldwide in scope and as diverse as the many cultural areas which it serves. The focus of these essays is on the challenge and the opportunity of building community, of forging a partnership between teachers, parents, administrative staff and friends of the school for the sake of the children and their development. It is an invitation to build community together as a seed for a new human-centered society of caring, of belonging and of mutual development.

Many of the nine essays in the book were written over the last twenty years, often as talks given at Waldorf conferences and events. They have been updated and modified to form a whole that I hope can be an inspiration and a help to the joys and struggles of building community among conscious and often opinionated adults. Many of the essays have benefited from the rich and enlivening dialogs that took place in the Waldorf School Administration and Community Development Program at Sunbridge College from 1993 to 2008. These conversations and shared case studies deepened my insights and caring, as have my many years of work in Waldorf school communities in this country and abroad.

The chapters can be read separately—with chapters 2–6 having a stronger practical focus, while chapters 1, 7, 8 and 9 have a more reflective philosophical orientation. The reader will, however, benefit from reading them in sequence. The more reflective essays contain many of Rudolf Steiner's social insights, which entered strongly into the founding of the first Waldorf school in Stuttgart, Germany, in 1919, and which have informed the history and traditions of the Waldorf School Movement since that time.

While the Waldorf School Movement is now over ninety years old, I believe its educational philosophy, its pedagogy and its social forms are still young and desperately needed in modern societies that increasingly educate for standardized tests, social compliance and the work force rather than for human and social creativity. I wholeheartedly agree with one commentator who, in describing the founding of the first Waldorf school in 1919, said that this first Waldorf school "was not begun as the idyllic refuge of wealthy esoterically-minded parents and their children, but as a healing impulse, as a healing initiative not only for the individual child but for all children, as the essence, hope and reality of a future society of peace." This then is our challenge in building Waldorf school communities: to educate children for the future, while creating a community of peace out of diversity, a community which honors the spirit and the uniqueness of each individual. I hope these essays can serve that end.

I

The Dialogue of Social Creation:
Practicing Social Art

Every person is a special kind of artist, and
every activity is a special art.
— M.C. Richards

As individuals we are faced with a host of social, economic
and political issues over which we appear to have little control. The
complexity of such questions and the burdens of everyday life can
combine to breed a feeling of powerlessness. Yet there is a realm in
which we can and do make a difference—the realm of social initiative,
of social creation. Whether we listen with an open heart to a teenage
boy talking about his fear; how we relate to our marriage partner; our
contributions at a faculty meeting; the manner in which we develop a
school, company or food cooperative—all make a difference. They are
all acts of social creation, which externalize something of our ideas and
values, of our being.[1]

The marvelous wisdom and beauty of the natural world is given
to us. We can admire it and seek to understand it, but it is not our
creation. The social world—that of Waldorf schools and of banks,
hospitals, highways, stores, living rooms, quarrels and laughter—is
our creation, no matter how objective, external and alien it may seem.
Each of us is involved in this ongoing social creation process, although
we seldom stop to think about it or to recognize its potential for
transformation. We are all social artists or, as M.C. Richards puts it,
"every person is a special kind of artist, and every activity is a special
art."[2] Being part of a Waldorf school community offers us a unique
opportunity to practice the art of social creation, to permeate our
relationship to the world of things, to others, to groups and to the
school community with a new consciousness.

The World of Things

If we accept the notion that we are all social artists, though often unconscious of our artistic activity and talent, questions arise about the nature, purpose, principles and areas of social art. Where does social art find expression? It seems to me that its most concrete manifestation is in our relation to the *world of things*—to tables, chairs, home decoration, classroom design, to how we button our shirt and set the table. My relation to the world of things hasn't been a particularly strong aspect of my social creativity, and yet, with prodding, I have learned to see that a beautifully set table affects mood, conversation and enjoyment at supper and that a clean and artistically decorated classroom helps learning.

Some friends of mine are involved in Camphill, curative educational communities for people with special needs. They so focus on the realm of things that children, co-workers and visitors experience a healing peace and harmony. This attention to the world of things, this mood of reverence for the everyday, is beautifully expressed by the English poet Paul Matthews.[3]

Things

What I'll miss most when I'm dead is
things that the light shines on.
If there aren't wet leaves in Heaven
Then almost I don't want to go there.
If there isn't the possibility
of silly particulars
like library cards on a table,
then almost I don't want to go there.
…
The Gods have enough of Immortality
and need things.
They need cuckoos in a damson tree.
They need rhubarbs flapping beside a gate.
Their paternoster is an honest man
who can hammer a nail straight.

The cherishing of daily life that is built into the Waldorf curriculum, into the verses and festivals and into the colors, shapes and objects of the classroom requires devotion, consciousness and a concern with beauty and rhythm. It can become an ongoing part of our awareness at home and in school.

Individual Relationships

A second area in which we practice social art is in our individual relationships—between teacher and student, between parents and between colleagues. A conversation is an artistic creation, as is a long-term relationship or a family. Interest, listening, responding and initiating are required when we engage in dialog. Is the conversation alive? Can I understand the feeling as well as the words? Do I respond in a way that engenders life, or am I in such a hurry that the exchange is simply functional? In our relationships in schools and in family life, do we seek mutual understanding and development? Do we grow and move beyond the habitual? Can we engender trust, love and commitment through thought and deed? This is a difficult area in which tiredness, prejudice and lack of awareness lead to habitual responses, to routine and to many non-artistic, deadening moments in relationships.

Groups

Who has not experienced faculty or Board meetings so boring that after ten minutes we execute a mental escape to some magical destination—visiting a friend or a possible location for next summer's vacation? For collegial institutions such as Waldorf schools, this area of social artistic expression is of great importance. The art of team building, of facilitating meetings so that mutual creativity is enhanced, is an area in which people do recognize the value of a socially aware artistic sensibility. The right thought, an encouraging comment, a good summary, intense listening or a joke—at appropriate moments—can add light and life to a meeting. As groups work over time, they can learn and grow by becoming more aware of the social creation process—of the joys and struggles in building creative work groups.

Communities and Organizations

A fourth area of social art is our involvement in the creation of communities and organizations. This is most obvious in the case of newly-created institutions. A couple I once knew in Montreal began selling futons (cotton mattresses) at street markets and soon had both a retail business and a small production facility; La Futonerie existed as a result of their ideas and creativity. Some twenty years ago a group of parents in an upstate New York community decided to create a Waldorf school, which is now thriving in a recently purchased former public elementary school. Five years ago a group of Waldorf graduates with young children met in Brooklyn and resolved to start a culturally and ethnically diverse school committed to sustainability. The Brooklyn Waldorf School is just about to move into its first proper home, leased from the Catholic Diocese of New York.

In each of these situations we see individuals engaged in creating something out of an idea and, if successful, meeting a human need for a product or service. Pioneers are usually realistic dreamers who enjoy the process of social creation—taking an idea and seeing it gradually take shape in matter—with co-workers, buildings and budgets.[4] Like sculptures and paintings, such creations externalize the founders' personalities, ideas, values and experiences.[5] Working with new schools, I often ask the founding teachers and parents to look at their strengths and weaknesses in order to see how their personality characteristics are imprinted on the organization, making visible the connection between personal development and organizational change.

The social art of creating new institutions is easier to see than that of developing established schools and communities. Yet the transition from the inspiring but tiring pioneer years to a more administratively oriented and secure next phase of development can be consciously and sensitively worked with so that founding teachers and parents feel honored. A change in location for the school or a necessary increase in tuition can be the cause either of bitter dispute or of clarifying community values, depending on how aware people are about the process.

That we as North Americans collectively create our culture—our world—can also be seen, although as I struggle my way through a mall, I may not be willing to acknowledge the connection. Lastly, our thoughts, feelings and acts are part of the fabric of the global community—the collective social creation of humanity.

What is it that we are creating and recreating as social artists both in Waldorf schools and in our local communities? The fabric of social life—the qualities and substance of a humanly created world which is increasingly replacing the natural world. Even more, we are becoming co-creators of our earthly universe—moving from dependence on nature to creating a world in which "Nature" is our servant. Is Rainer Maria Rilke right when he asks, "Earth, is it not just this that you want—to arise invisibly in us?"[6] These answers are at best partial, a beginning in comprehending the reality that we are creating a new cosmos woven out of our physical, psychological and spiritual capacities. The humanly created social world is replacing nature as the primary focus of human experience.

The substance, the medium of this art of social creation is our own nature—the combination of soul and spirit qualities we bring into the creative process. The main requirement of social art, as with all arts, is that we are aware and willing to enter into the demands of the present situation. As M.C. Richards notes, "We are artists so long as we are alive to the concreteness of a moment and do not use it to some other purpose."[7]

This requirement is not simple. It asks first that we be truly present with our awareness; second, that we perceive what is asked, needed or possible in this situation; and third, that we respond in helpful or appropriate ways. This creative process, so central to the life of Waldorf school communities, is complicated by the fact that it takes place between two or more people, each with his or her own thoughts, feelings and intentions shaped by past experiences. And so through inattention, worry or lack of time we often don't manage very well. In the middle of a conversation in the hall I realize I'm not present, worrying about my phone call in five minutes. Or at a staff meeting I frantically raise my arm wanting to be heard, thereby no longer listening to a colleague who is speaking. Yet if brought to consciousness, we learn from both the artistic and inartistic acts of social creation.

The Mirror and the Invitation

In the arts we have choices in how we sculpt a form or what colors we use. In social art this is also true: what word, what gesture, what deed. We can then step back, look at what we have created, and learn. Reflection on the social creation process can stimulate self-development in two main ways: as a mirror and as an invitation. A conversation, meeting, relationship or school mirrors our individual and joint soul states. It is also an invitation to individual and collective development, to transformation—if we acknowledge that we have created the group, the school, and that they reflect our nature, and that we can learn from how things are.

How does the *mirror function* work? Reflection on our relationships in Waldorf schools reveals aspects of the self-centered, antisocial nature of modern consciousness. Indeed the collegial structure of Waldorf schools often enhances tensions between people, as we cannot rely on hierarchy or power to resolve differences of opinion. I remember working with one school where differences about how to work with adolescents expanded to include gender issues and spiritual orientation. As neither party took responsibility for the conflict, shifting the burden of blame to the other, and the faculty as a whole did not feel fully responsible for guiding a resolution process, this conflict did great damage to the school community over a number of years.

If we pay careful attention to our thought life when listening to one another, we can observe the functioning of critical intelligence, of doubt: "Yes, but have you thought of…? I don't think that's correct," and we have stopped listening to assert our ideas and opinions. Or, if we don't like something about an institution we work in, we adopt a critical mood, not seeking to understand the institution or its culture, focus or aim.

If we turn to our feelings, we notice strong likes and dislikes, antipathies and sympathies. "Consensus doesn't really work, does it?" "Martha is a likable but disorganized class teacher." "Those parents don't understand children…" These likes and dislikes do tell us how we feel, but being strongly colored by projections or moods, they often don't give us a real picture of the other or of the situation. Strong sympathies and antipathies, like doubt and criticism, close us off from the social world, making it difficult to perceive what is really going on and responding in helpful ways.

If we stop and reflect on our behavior and intentions in a group, in a relationship, or in the broader Waldorf community, we can notice how pleased we are when we get our way and how we react in a variety of negative ways when we don't. At this more subtle will level of the soul, we can become aware of a certain selfishness, of egotism.

By paying attention we can recognize three important antisocial qualities in ourselves and in our communities: doubt and criticism in our thought life; likes and dislikes in our feeling life; and egotism and selfishness in our will. These qualities find expression in the parking lot rumor mill, the latent or overt staff conflicts and in smaller ways in the myriad of interactions which make up the Waldorf school community. Recognizing these antisocial qualities can become a powerful call to self-development, to inner transformation. This is the mirror function of social creation, of community life. It is only by being genuinely and actively engaged with others that we meet the shadow side of ourselves, the limitations of self that require work.[8]

Social life also offers an invitation to develop interest, empathy and, ultimately, love and compassion. Such an invitation is subtle and requires a daily review of our relationships and work life. But if we can overcome doubt and criticism and become really interested in a child, a colleague or a class, this can lead to understanding and to healing and helpful acts.

In my conflict resolution work in Waldorf schools, I often recommend that two people who are having difficulties tell each other their life stories. This usually moves people from criticism and animosity to a certain level of interest and understanding: The other is no longer an object, but a struggling human being like myself.

Interest in another or in a social situation is only the beginning. It is that which opens us to the questions: What is going on? Who is that person? Interest leads to the desire for deeper understanding, to empathy. How did this situation arise? Why do I have difficulty with this colleague? What makes him act this way at meetings? As we gain understanding and insight, we identify ourselves with the person, the situation or the group—it is us, not them. In meetings, we can experience this very directly—the antisocial quality of removing ourselves, of judging: We are not responsible for this, What a waste of time, Why does she take so long to speak? The moment we become interested in the meeting or understand the difficulty between two colleagues, or between that parent and that teacher, then we have opened our heart.

The mirror and the invitation in social life can be portrayed in the following manner:

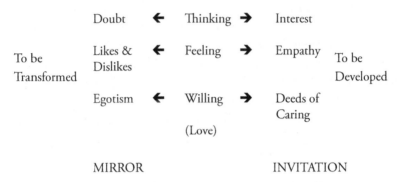

	Doubt	←	Thinking →	Interest	
To be Transformed	Likes & Dislikes	←	Feeling →	Empathy	To be Developed
	Egotism	←	Willing →	Deeds of Caring	
			(Love)		

MIRROR   INVITATION

Social Art and Social Inquiry in Everyday Life

Reflecting on our involvement in the social creation process not only tells us about the qualities of our individual and collective consciousness, but it is also the beginning of social science. By stepping back and reviewing a group process, a successful development campaign in a school or a conflict, we can learn about the laws of social creation.

Every art has its scientific counterpart. The laws of color or form need to be understood by the painter or sculptor; the laws of social creation need to be explored and increasingly understood by us all. By thinking about specific social situations, we can understand the underlying principles, for example: that group development and team-building require clear goals and a deepening level of trust; that all social creations reflect and are supported by the "subjective" dimension of our consciousness; that groups and organizations go through stages of development which can be described and worked on; that new institutions require the attention and sacrifice of their founders before they can respond effectively to the individual needs of co-workers.[9]

In daily life we move continuously between moments of social art and social inquiry. For example, we come to a finance committee meeting to help decide on a request for a salary increase. Do we listen seriously to the request, understanding its background and motives? We interact with other colleagues and exchange opinions. We arrive at a decision. The decision affects the individual and the budget of a whole institution; it is a series of *social artistic acts*. Later, we reflect on the decision process: How did we arrive at this decision; what does it say about our decision-making process; how does the decision reflect our institution's values and policies? This is a reflective moment of *social* inquiry. Perhaps through it we understand that an effective collegial decision-making process always requires a stage in which individual values and criteria for judgment are shared before a consensus can be reached.

As we deepen our social understanding, our ability to function intuitively and effectively as social artists increases. True social concepts deepen perception and fire the will. Conversely, becoming a more conscious social artist increases the desire for deeper social understanding.

In ancient times, the royal art was that of temple building; now and in the future, the highest art will be that of social creation. We are only at the beginning of this recognition, and at the beginning of true and conscious social science. The practice of social art and social inquiry in everyday life is what we all share as human beings, but it must be taken out of the realm of instinct and impulse and be consciously practiced if we are to build a better society.[10] Practicing social art and developing social understanding is one of the great gifts of participating in the building of Waldorf school communities. This practice, present in all social relationships, means bridging the social threshold between myself and another, developing interest and beginning to work with love. Brenda Ueland, a writer and journalist, suggests that conscious listening is such a practice. "We should all know this: that listening, not talking, is the gifted and great role, and the imaginative role. And the true listener is much more beloved, magnetic than the talker, and he (she) is more effective, and learns more and does more good. And so try listening. ... It will work a small miracle. And perhaps work a great one."[11]

Chapter I Reflection & Exercises:

Important Meetings and Conversations:

Call to mind two or three important meetings and conversations from your life.

- ☐ Who were you meeting?
- ☐ What was the setting?
- ☐ What did the conversation feel like?
- ☐ In what way did you feel met?
- ☐ What did the conversation or meeting lead to?

What have you learned about yourself?

- ☐ From working with others in groups?
- ☐ From your close relationships?

An Aid to Meeting One on One, and a Biographical Reflection from Rudolf Steiner:

Dyad Work (Two People)

- ☐ Face another person, looking at him and he at you.
- ☐ Ask (Carol, Michael): Who are you?
- ☐ The person speaks uninterrupted for five minutes.
- ☐ Then he asks you: Who are you?
- ☐ You speak for five minutes uninterrupted.
- ☐ Repeat the exercise for another round.
- ☐ Share what you have experienced in doing the exercise.

LEVELS OF LISTENING
Helps and Hindrances

To be effective listeners, we must learn to listen to the whole person—not just to the words he/she is saying, but also to what lies between or behind the actual words. We need to listen to thoughts, feelings, and intentions.

> *"Head listening" to facts, concepts, arguments, ideas.*
> *"Heart listening" to emotions, values, mood, experience.*
> *"Listening to the will" energy, direction, motivation.*

The Thinking Level: Head Listening

This is the most obvious way to listen—apparently "objective"—but not as effective as we imagine. Can we truly follow with our own thoughts, the thoughts of the speaker? We think much faster than he/she speaks. How do we use this extra mental time? To synthesize and digest what we are hearing, or to think our own separate thoughts?

Hindrances on this level include problems of attention and accuracy, but also arise from the different frames of reference held by speaker and listener. Our knowledge, concepts, vocabulary and way of thinking derive from the past—our own individual past education and experience. If we do not allow for the fact that the other person has his own, perhaps very different, frame of reference, it is all too easy to get our wires crossed, or to assume a level of understanding that is not real. We continually run the danger of over-complicating or over-simplifying what we hear.

The listening process is supported on this level by the cultivation of a genuine interest in "where the other person is coming from"—an open-minded approach that does not judge his/her words according to my preconceptions.

The Feeling Level: Heart Listening

Listening on this level means penetrating a step deeper into the other's experience. Apparently rational statements may be covering feelings of distress, anger or embarrassment. These may be heard more through the tone of voice, facial expressions or a gesture than in what is actually said, and can be obscured, especially if we are unaccustomed to, or inhibited about, expressing feelings directly.

Accurate perception of feelings is continually impaired by the effects of our own feelings, the likes and dislikes that arise in us semiconsciously in the face of certain people, situations or issues. Even the mention of certain "trigger" words or phrases can call up quite strong emotions in us, which obscure our perception of what the other is feeling. Effective listening can be fostered on the feeling left by "quieting" our own reactions to the immediate impressions we receive and developing the quality of empathy. This means allowing ourselves calmly to "live into" the other person's experience as he/she is speaking.

The faculty of social sensibility that can be trained in this way is a key attribute of skilled negotiators.

The Will Level: Intentional Listening

To sense the real intentions of another person can be one of the hardest aspects of the art of listening. Often, speakers are themselves only dimly aware of what they actually want in a situation. Skillful listening can help to discover, "behind" the thoughts and "below" the feelings involved, the real sources of potential energy and commitment. This will often involve sensing what is left unsaid. The future lies asleep in people's will-forces.[12]

Listening on Three Levels

AIM: To practice skills of listening in the following ways:
1) Accuracy and attention in relation to the information, ideas and mental pictures actually expressed by the speaker
2) Sensitivity to the underlying feelings and mood, which may or may not be directly expressed
3) Recognizing the fundamental direction of the speaker's intentions and energy

METHOD: In groups of four, one person relates a recent experience that contains a certain problem or question for him/her, which is still open or unresolved. Each listener takes one level. After the speaker has finished and a brief pause for reflection, the listeners are asked to share their observations in the following ways respectively:
1) Retell in your own words the main elements of the story you heard. What facts and concepts did the speaker use to make that situation clear?
2) Describe the feelings you imagine were present in the speaker:
   a) in the past situation that was described, and
   b) during the telling.
3) What kinds of motivation could you perceive in the speaker? What does/did he/she want to do about the situation described? How much commitment and energy is present, and in what directions?

All observations are then checked with the storyteller. How accurate was the listening? What was missed? Did the feedback make the speaker more aware of certain semiconscious factors? Distinguish between observation and interpretation—how justified was the latter?

Repeat with new tellers, possibly also with listeners all taking all levels, building up feedback together on each.[13]

Using Nonviolent Communication as an Aid in Potentially Difficult Conversations

We are often in situations at work or at home when we feel hurt, ostracized or misunderstood by another or when we wish another to alter his/her behavior in our presence. In these situations it is useful to employ the distinctions and language which lie at the heart of Marshall Rosenberg's work in Nonviolent Communication. The important distinctions to be aware of are:

1) What behavior do we actually observe?
2) What effect does this behavior have on our feelings? (Feeling)
3) What are our needs and values which underlie, create our feelings? (Thinking)
4) What specific actions do we request from the other? (Willing)

These distinctions can be useful but if used routinely as a methodology can also lead to egotism—"I need to have my needs met"—as can any psychological or communication technique. If we actually use it with others, we need to also be open to the other, to practice heartfelt listening.[14]

Endnotes

1. See P. Berger and T. Luckman, *The Social Construction of Reality: A Treatise in the Sociology of Knowledge* (Doubleday, New York, 1966).

2. M.C. Richards, *Centering: In Pottery, Poetry and Person* (Wesleyan University Press, Middletown, CT, 1964), pp. 46–47.

3. O. Davis and P. Matthews, *Two Stones, One Bird* (Smith Doorstop Books, Huddersfield, England, 1988).

4. See C. Schaefer and T. Voors, *Vision in Action: Working with Soul and Spirit in Small Organizations* (Lindisfarne Press, Hudson, NY, 1996), pp. 59–102.

5. Op. cit., Berger and Luckman; they see institutions as a kind of objective distillation of people's ideas and values, a perspective which conforms to my experience.

6. R.M. Rilke, *Duino Elegies* (Hogarth Press, London, 1963).

7. Op. cit., Richards, p. 46.

8. Rudolf Steiner, *Social and Anti-Social Forces in the Human Being* (Mercury Press, Spring Valley, NY, 1986).

9. See Schaefer and Voors, op. cit., for a description of the phases of organization and community development; also Chapter II of this book.

10. Rudolf Steiner, *Awakening to Community* (Anthroposophic Press, Hudson, NY, 1986).

11. Brenda Ueland, "Tell Me More: On the Fine Art of Listening" (*Utne Reader*, Nov/Dec 1992). Also, Steve Briault, in *The Mystery of Meeting: Relationships as a Path of Discovery* (Sophia Books, Forest Row, UK, 2010), provides a moving and rich exploration of relationships in family life and at work.

12. Op. cit., Schaefer and Voors, pp. 106–107.

13. Ibid., p. 109.

14. See Marshall Rosenberg, *Nonviolent Communication: A Language of Compassion* (Puddle Press, Encinitas, CA, 1999), in particular pp. 1–37.

II

Phases of Waldorf School Development

*Every living being is in process, which is simply the flow, the
stream of its life journey. Such processes are both archetypal—
sharing commonality of pattern with all beings, such as
gestation, birth, death and resurrection—as well as unique to
the particular being. Individuals and social organisms (groups,
organizations and communities) endowed with the gift of
(self) consciousness have the possibility of becoming aware of
their own processes, and thus become responsible for their own
evolution.* [1]

– Allan Kaplan

This description of school development gives a general picture of
characteristic phases in the life cycle of a Waldorf school.[2] It is meant
to provide a perspective or guide to aid faculty, administration and
parents, as well as Board members to more consciously develop their
school. The picture presented in no way seeks to deny the uniqueness of
each individual Waldorf school's biography, but rather to point toward
characteristic questions and issues which exist in the life history of most
schools.[3]

Underlying this description of the life cycle of Waldorf schools
are a number of principles. The first is that all institutions are human
creations; they are created by people with an idea in response to a
perceived need. In the case of Waldorf schools, this need is a sense that
the children in a given community or region want Waldorf education.
The second principle is that schools, and indeed all organizations,
are living entities, with phases of adaptation, growth, crisis and
development.[4] This means that organic metaphors such as seed, stalk,
bud and flower; or birth childhood, adulthood and old age are more
relevant to the biography of schools than mechanical images such as

that of an input-output system, a clockwork mechanism or a well-running engine. In creating a school we are indeed creating a living being, whose destiny may be unknown to us, but which requires our love and ongoing commitment to flourish.

A third principle, and one which I find to be crucial, is that there is no one right form for all Waldorf schools. There are, of course, relevant principles in forming a Waldorf school, such as the idea of a collegial institution or that of phases in the life cycle of a school. But ultimately, each group of teachers, parents, children and friends must evolve those particular forms which can most effectively express their intentions. A consequence of this principle is that school forms need to evolve and change over time in order to reflect new human and spiritual aspirations.

Working with these principles leads to a presentation of characteristic issues and developmental questions rather than specific answers. Questions bring consciousness, and consciousness is that which determines the social forms we create and how well we work with them.

Birth and Childhood: Improvising in Response to Needs

The birth of a Waldorf school has its origins in the deep commitment of one or more individuals to the ideals of Waldorf education. Such a commitment may arise through visiting an existing school, or by reading a book on Waldorf education, or through hearing an inspiring lecture. The ideals of the education light up, and an individual or a small group may say, "This community needs a Waldorf school and I am going to work on it!" This lighting up, this moment of conception, happens in a great variety of ways. It is always interesting to go back in a school's history and find out who first conceived the imagination of the school and under what circumstances it arose. One founding personality read Rudolf Steiner's name in a book while on a plane. He then ordered many of Rudolf Steiner's lectures and was struck by those given to teachers and so resolved to start a school for English children in the U.S. in the middle of World War II. This school later became the Kimberton Waldorf School. In another, quite common circumstance, a group of potential parents met at a presentation on

Waldorf education, began to study A.C. Harwood's book, *The Recovery of Man in Childhood*, and decided to start a school.[5] A third common founding experience is that of a trained Waldorf teacher who moves to a community and resolves to start a school, such as was the case of the Pine Hill Waldorf School in Wilton, New Hampshire.

Following the moment of conception is a period of gestation or pregnancy in which one or more individuals are walking around carrying this idea. This gestation period will vary in time. The Toronto Waldorf School had a long preparation period; other school groups begin a kindergarten after only one or two years of preparation. During this preparation time, lectures and workshops are organized, fairs are given and the world is being told about the initiative, about the child one hopes to bring into the world. It is at times a frightening process involving many inner and outer questions, to name a few:

Who is really committed to the school?

What is our understanding of Waldorf education and anthroposophy?

How much money will we need?

What are the right legal forms?

Do we create a Waldorf School Association as a non-profit organization?

How do we find an experienced or a trained Waldorf teacher?

How will we know when to start?

These and other questions need conscious attention before the kindergarten or school opens its doors. A central issue is whether one has the intention of developing a kindergarten and a grade school or just a kindergarten. Developing a kindergarten and a grade school together or in a short sequence has many advantages, but requires a deeper and more sustaining commitment. Equally important is the question of motive. Does the initiative group consist mainly of parents who want the school for their own children? What happens when the school or kindergarten takes a year or two longer to develop than anticipated? A core group of people whose commitment goes beyond their immediate, personal interest is essential.

Another issue is whether there is enough actual or anticipated support. Are there enough children to begin with grade one and add another grade each year? Does the region have a population adequate to support a school?

In working with very young schools or with school initiative groups, I have found seven question areas developed by my colleague Tÿno Voors to be most helpful. They provide a kind of checklist for clarification which can help new school groups and other new initiatives avoid many of the difficulties which new ventures face in the first few years of their existence.[6]

A Checklist of Questions and Issues for New Schools

1. Recognizing the Vision

   What is our imagination, our vision for this school?
   Do we have a common image?
   What ideas do we hope to realize?
   How do we relate to Waldorf education and to anthroposophy?
   What changes will the school bring about in our lives, in our
       children's lives, and in the community?

2. Answering a Need

   Is there a need for a Waldorf school in our community, and how do
       we know this?
   Are there sufficient numbers of children and parents interested in
       Waldorf education?
   What needs and wishes does the community express about
       education?
   What do these expressions of interest say about the opportunities
       and limitations we face in starting a Waldorf school?

3. Formulating a Direction

   What will be the name of the school?
   What image of the school do we wish to promote and realize over
       the next two to three years?

What activities will we foster over the next few years to nurture and support the school?

What kind of brochure should we have?

4. Commitment of People

Who is committed to the initiative and why?

Who is in the initiative group and who can be counted on for the long haul?

Who are the supporters?

Is the general community aware and supportive of the school?

Is there financial support?

5. Organizing Our Work Together

What are the right legal forms for us?

How are we going to organize the school, the association, the Board, faculty and parent group?

Who will make what decisions and how will decisions be communicated between various groups?

How will we relate to supporters, Board members, parent community and town?

What financial arrangements will we make for tuition income and for salaries?

6. Work Activities

What are the central work activities needed in the school: teaching, office, public relations, fundraising, etc?

What are our priorities?

Who will do what?

How will work be coordinated and by whom?

What do we see as volunteer work and what as paid work?

7. Finding Facilities and Resources

What building space and equipment will we need now and in three to five years?

What quality of environment do we wish to create for children and teachers?

Do we have a capital budget?

Do we have the intention of building a new school or buying an existing one?

How are we going to deal with the usual operating deficit of the first few years?

Is there a fundraising and development committee?

Do we have a development plan for the future?

New school groups are usually stronger in certain areas than in others. One has a strong sense of public relations, another for building a strong group, a third a good sense of financial and administrative clarity. Working with questions such as these can help to identify areas which have been neglected and now need attention.

Following the gestation period is the exciting moment of birth, when the school or kindergarten opens its door and the children arrive for the first time. This is a very important moment in the biography of any institution and should be celebrated accordingly. A foundation ceremony, a birthday celebration, in which teachers, parents, children, friends and visitors can participate, should be planned. In this way one invites both the visible and the invisible world to bless and support that which has been inaugurated.

If the new school flourishes, it enters a period analogous to childhood—vibrant, exciting and, of course, full of surprises. It is a time of ups and downs, of mood swings and crises. "Will we have enough money to meet payroll?" Yet, it is also a time of blessing, of unforeseen help. I remember sitting with other parents at a new school in the Boston area that was to become the Waldorf School in Lexington, wondering about how we could cover the next month's payroll, when an anonymous donation of $2000 arrived.

Generally people have a high level of motivation and much warmth toward the fledgling school because they are participating in a marvelous creation process. First there was an idea, carried by a few people, but no children, teachers, money and no building. To see one's own dream then gradually begin to incarnate is a wonderful, if tiring, experience.

As the new school grows it manifests a number of characteristic qualities which it shares with other new initiatives.

- It is generally of small to medium size—a kindergarten and a few grades or perhaps even up to grade six.

- It has a shallow, informal organizational form with a limited hierarchy. Perhaps there are three sets of founding couples and two founding teachers who jointly make important decisions over a kitchen table or in a church basement.

- Leadership in the school is personal, direct and informal. New teachers and new parents may take some time to fit in because there is a personal style of doing things. If one doesn't like this style or the personalities of those in the carrying group, social difficulties frequently follow.

- Decision making is largely intuitive rather than analytical. Things are decided more by hunch or by feel than through lengthy analysis. Hiring is based on a feeling that this person will fit in and this person won't.

- The young school has a family atmosphere about it. Everyone contributes as he or she is able, and most teachers, staff members and families have a strong sense of loyalty to the school and a sense of camaraderie toward each other. Later this sense of informal cohesion dissipates and people speak longingly of the old days, of painting classrooms together, of endless weeks preparing for the fair or of the struggle to find enough money to buy desks.

- The goals and direction of the new school are largely implicit, carried in the minds and hearts of the carrying group of founding teachers and parents. This is not to say that Waldorf education is not talked about, but rather that spelling out in detail the many aspects of what kind of a Waldorf school it will be is rightly seen as unnecessary. It would be a bit like asking a seven-year-old to tell you with precision what he or she would want to do when grown up.[7]

Childhood Illnesses

In the same way that children have childhood diseases, new schools face challenges and difficulties analogous to bouts of illness. They are seldom fatal, and they can serve to strengthen the school if worked with. A few of the more common childhood illnesses of new Waldorf schools are:

- The pioneer godparent, who wants a Waldorf school, helps it to get started and partially funds the initiative, but is not existentially involved. The help often comes with strings attached, and the person may seek to control the hiring and development of the school. While the motives are usually positive, unless the person actually works in the school and gradually gives up his or her authority to a faculty group and Board, endless difficulties ensue.

- The golden spoon is a similar difficulty. If one or two people fund an initiative, automatically covering its deficits, then the school never has to articulate its purpose and generate support from a wider parent and community group. This situation is analogous to being excessively pampered—it spoils one and leads to not facing reality.

- The over-planned and "perfect Waldorf school" where everything is so planned out that the reality of the local setting and its needs are never seen or heard. Such an orientation creates a school incapable of responding to needs and opportunities, a school too rigid and ideological to have a living dialog with children, parents and environment.

- The reverse of the "perfect Waldorf school" is a new school whose commitment to Waldorf education is so loose that it becomes an alternative school, attempting to cater to the wishes of a very diverse parent community. Sooner or later this creates an atmosphere where no one is happy since each group has a different picture of what the school should be.

- The perfect home syndrome in which a young school group finds the ideal site, suitable for the next seven years, but quite expensive, and spends all its human and financial energy on the site before the school is actually established.

- The balanced sharing of responsibility in the life of a school is one of the most common areas of conflict as a school grows. If the school was started by a strong parent group, there is the need to give a growing teacher body responsibility for all areas of the pedagogy, including hiring. If it was started by teachers, the challenge is one of creating a Board and parent association which have real involvement in areas of finance, publicity, outreach and a host of other areas necessary to support the education. In either case, it is a question of learning to openly share responsibility for the well-being of the initiative.

As these and other developmental difficulties are overcome, the school will grow in strength and size. Above all, it will begin to feel as if it is here to stay. The early dramas of enrollment, teacher recruitment and financial deficit still appear, but one doesn't have the feeling that they are life-threatening. Indeed after five, six, seven or more years, a sense of continuity, of growth and confidence exists in most schools.

A Time of Transition

A period of "relative" tranquility, of an understood order and way of doing things, may go on for quite a number of years. Yet as the initiative grows, with six, seven or eight grades, a new group of questions and concerns appears. Partly this is connected to size; with over 150 children and many full- and part-time teachers, the old feeling of intimacy disappears. New teachers and parents join the school who have not shared the joys and struggles of the early days and who have no relation to the school's past or to many of the people who made the school what it is. Indeed, they begin to resent the myths and sagas of the heroic old days.

In many schools this transition phase from childhood to adulthood manifests itself through a typical set of issues. One of these is a loss of confidence in existing leadership. Criticism is heard, usually from newer teachers or parents, about the "autocratic," "arbitrary" or "irrational" manner in which decisions are made. Such criticism also points to unclarity about goals, policies and direction. Earlier in the history of the school, there was a direct, personal relationship between members of the school community. Most people knew who to go to when an issue arose. As this breaks down, a need for clearly articulated goals and policies is perceived, and in their absence, questions likely to arise are: What are the disciplinary procedures in the school? How is teacher hiring and evaluation carried out? What roles do Board and parents play in the establishment of the budget?

A connected question which arises in this transitional time is the nature of teacher-parent relationships. If the faculty of a Waldorf school carries full educational responsibility for the curriculum, for teaching activities and for teacher hiring and evaluation, what is the role of the parent in the life of a school? How does a parent move from being interested in the school and supporting Waldorf education to being a member of the Finance Committee or the Board of Trustees?

Another frequently expressed concern is the inadequacy of administrative practices. In the early years, parents, teachers, spouses and friends helped in the office, answered phones and carried out a large variety of administrative work. Now the workload and the need for more adequate records and for financial expertise require more help. The call for professionalism of office and administration is indeed a need which requires a number of full- and part-time people, preferably with both a deep understanding of Waldorf education and experience in financial and administrative matters.

These issues, and others in combination, produce a crisis of confidence that is both perplexing and painful for the school community. As in adolescence, the need for change and development is recognized, but its direction appears obscure. It is in such circumstances that developmental pictures can help, not as a prescription, but as a perspective which outlines the contours of the next possible landscape.

Adulthood: Differentiation with Clarity

The challenge in this phase of a school's development is how to achieve greater clarity and a better division of responsibility so that a larger, more complex organization can thrive. In the early years, getting started and surviving was paramount. Now, it is permeating the school's life with a new consciousness, which allows more functional differentiation, without sacrificing individual creativity and commitment. I believe that achieving this balance and entering a healthy differentiation process involves paying attention to a number of interconnected elements, some of which have already been touched on.

One important need for the school at this stage of its evolution is renewing its identity and purpose by developing a shared vision of the future and a clear mission statement. This means a renewed dialog with the original intention, with the spirit of the school. What was our original vision and what is it now? Do we wish to develop a full Waldorf school K–12 or just K–8? It is not enough to say we want a Waldorf school now, but what kind of a Waldorf school, with what qualities, and in what setting. To involve faculty, Board, parents and friends in a longer discussion of the future can focus the will and generate enthusiasm toward the work needing to be done.[8]

In addition to a picture of the future and a mission statement, the faculty and Board of the school need to become clearer about policies so that a division and delegation of responsibilities can occur. As schools move into this phase of development, committees proliferate. Yet, frequently they are not allowed to really work since the faculty or the College of Teachers wants to be involved in every decision. This is not the result of perversity, but rather that committees do not have access to clearly articulated policies on the host of issues affecting the life of the school. Policies are statements of value preference, and they should have the full support of the faculty and, in many cases, the Board. For example: What is the basis for teacher salaries? Is an experienced teacher with Waldorf training a priority? Is a part of the policy on teacher hiring to inquire about the relation to anthroposophy? What are the policies on scholarships, on expulsion, on drug use? Is there a clear policy on teacher evaluation and development? Each of these areas requires value judgments. If these judgments have not been *discussed, agreed to and embodied in policies, a committee has no basis for action.* To my mind, the absence of clear policies undermines the vitality and life of many Waldorf schools because it means that committees cannot work and that both faculty and College meetings are clogged up with a multitude of detailed issues which limit pedagogical and spiritual work.

As mentioned, an important principle in this phase of school development is that of giving clear tasks to committees and individuals.[9] If policies have been established, then the function, tenure and reporting responsibilities of committees can be defined and a form of *republican leadership, of delegated responsibilities*, exercised.[10] The following types of committees are common in most established Waldorf schools:

Faculty	Board
Pedagogical Committee	Finance and Budget
Enrollment	Tuition Assistance
Hiring and Teacher Evaluation	Long-Term Planning
Festivals and Special Events	Development
Administrative Committee	Buildings and Grounds

Republican leadership (I am, of course, not talking about political parties) requires trust, or at least the discipline of letting others do a task differently than you would have done it. To do so runs counter to the democratic urge to be involved in everything. Rudolf Steiner hoped that by sharing leadership responsibilities among the teachers in the first Waldorf school in Stuttgart, mutual support and a new school spirit would be generated, but he was often disappointed as cliques, rivalries and ill-will were as much a danger then as now.[11]

Another aspect of the need for functional specialization and clarifying structural relationships is the necessity of refining the roles and relationships of the main decision-making bodies in the life of the school. In most Waldorf schools this includes the College of Teachers, the Administrative Council, the Faculty Meeting, the Board of Trustees, and the Parent-Teacher Association. Clarifying parent-teacher relationships is part of this task. In many Waldorf schools the quality of teacher-parent relations has not received sufficient attention, which leads to unnecessary misunderstandings and conflicts.[12]

An additional dimension of the differentiation phase in the life of a school is the need for a change in leadership and decision-making styles. In most new schools leadership is personal and decisions are made by hunch, based on a kind of intuition. As the school grows, leadership needs to become more functionally related to areas of expertise and responsibility. People need to be asked to take on different leadership responsibilities based on competence, not on who is willing to do it. A volunteer principle is appropriate in the early years of a school's life, but no longer when it is well-established. The Board Chair, the School Treasurer, the Faculty and College Chairs should, for example, all be selected based on an understanding of the job and on an awareness of the personal qualities and job skills of potential nominees.

At the same time, decision making needs greater rationality and consciousness. Both leadership and decision making will develop over time, but the transition is often difficult as individuals used to the freer, less defined approach of the early years resent the more rational and sometimes more "bureaucratic" approach of the differentiation phase.

If the above-mentioned needs of renewed vision, clearer policies, differentiated structures and committee systems and a transformed style of leadership and decision making are met, then the school can enter a healthy differentiation process in which new forms are balanced by a new, more "administrative" consciousness. Many Waldorf schools resist meeting these administrative questions, either because of limited organizational experience or because teachers do not have the time, energy or inclination to come to grips with these types of issues. In the same way that early adulthood calls on a different awareness than adolescence, so too will the complexity of a growing school require a greater organizational awareness. When the school enters the differentiation phase, as many of the older Waldorf schools have, it manifests some or all of the following qualities:

1. Increased size and complexity
2. Clearer policies and procedures
3. Differentiated structures, with a clear committee system
4. A higher level of expertise and more specialization and professionalism in administrative areas
5. More functional leadership, with a greater dispersal of responsibilities
6. More rational modes of decision making
7. Greater clarity of work activities

One can view a school as a living being requiring the maintenance of three dialogs for its health. The first dialog is with the spirit, with the ideals of Waldorf education and with the spiritual being of the school. The second necessary dialog is with the human and social environment: with parents, children and friends and with the community. The third dialog is with the earth: with finances, administration, buildings and grounds. The administrative focus of the differentiation phases emphasizes the dialog with the earth, and this emphasis must be consciously balanced by paying attention to spiritual ideals and to human relationships.[13]

The phase of differentiation may go on for many years in a school's life. Its emphasis on clarity and rationality suggests that this period is analogous to early and middle adulthood.

The long-term limitations of an administrative phase, when attention and consciousness is rightly focused inwardly, are very visible to those individuals working in large corporations and governmental bureaucracies. But they also manifest in older Waldorf schools, in hospitals and other smaller but well-established institutions. The weight of the past and of tradition, the number of endless meetings, a lack of purpose and leadership, communication difficulties, the absence of innovation and a growing sense of mediocrity are the most common concerns. Being well-established and in most cases quite secure, it is as if the school were experiencing a kind of mid-life crisis, in which the search for new meaning and a new way of working becomes critical.

Maturity: A Conscious Community of Learning, Meeting and Service

Bernhard Lievegoed refers to the third major phase of a school's or a cultural organization's life as a time of flowering.[14] To bring about such a flowering, I believe, requires meeting three major challenges if the school is to avoid the dangers of mediocrity and decline. These challenges are now not so much external as internal. Usually the school will own its buildings and have reasonable enrollment and a certain level of financial stability. It will also have developed traditions and habits which are both assets and liabilities.

The first challenge is that of becoming *a conscious learning community*. A teaching culture runs the risk of being devoted to knowledge acquired in the past and to imparting that knowledge to others. While this is indeed essential, over time we can become comfortable and not open to new inquiry. We may even resent other Waldorf schools' efforts to work with the grade school curriculum or with adolescents differently than we do. The first part of becoming a conscious learning community involves deepening the spiritual, meditative and pedagogical work of teachers. Can we bring to consciousness and renew our commitment to the path of individual inner development and to the principles of Waldorf education? Can faculty or college meetings create time for individual teachers to explore with others what is working for them and what is not? Indeed this is what Rudolf Steiner had in mind: the creation of a teacher academy for mutual learning and development. Strengthening and enlivening the joint meditations of teachers in the college meeting is also very important.

A part of becoming a conscious learning community is to inaugurate a conscious professional development plan for all teachers and staff. Can the school every year ask each teacher and full-time staff person to develop a personal and professional development plan in which the goals of inner and outer development are articulated and shared? Such goals could be shared briefly in the faculty-staff meeting and worked with in more detail within the personnel committee. The visits of master teachers and the attendance at professional conferences and workshops would then have a conscious and integrated learning and development focus.

Another aspect of becoming a conscious learning community is to develop a conscious learning and review process for all organs of the school's life. As all development activities require extra effort and consciousness, perhaps a Learning Mandate group could be established to coordinate and stimulate activity. Do the mandate groups and committees have a conscious learning and review process? A good pattern is to briefly review or evaluate every meeting. Have we achieved our aims? What was the mood of our gathering, how was speaking and listening? This need not be more than five minutes, although in form it needs to be consciously varied in order to avoid boredom and routine. Every semester a longer review of functioning can be established. How is the Finance Committee working? What are the strengths and weaknesses of the faculty and staff meeting? What can we do to improve things? This applies to the Board, the parent association and the faculty and staff. Then every year, perhaps after the close of school, a Learning Forum could be held to assess the achievements and limitations of the year. Parents, Board, friends, faculty and staff could participate in a kind of learning festival in which different aspects of the school's life can be explored for learning and improvement. In any type of learning effort, the mood is not one of blaming, but of saying what we can learn from these successes and these failures. This type of annual retreat can generate hope, for it allows the naming of issues but with the purpose of improvement, learning, and growth.

A Culture of Partnership

The second major challenge of becoming a mature school community is to develop a *true culture of partnership and of meeting*. A school is a destiny community of children, teachers, parents, staff and supporters. How can this recognition find form and substance? The first requirement is that we consciously recognize this destiny partnership and honor it. At the heart of this question is the relationship between teachers and children, staff, and parents. The teachers give their knowledge, care and love of the education and of the child; the administration supports the education and makes it possible practically; the parents entrust their children and, in the case of Waldorf schools in North America, provide the financial resources to support the education. This relationship finds expression in the organs of the school's life, in the College of Teachers, in the faculty/ staff meeting, in the School Association, in the Board and in class evenings. Can the partnership be made fully conscious in agreements on rights and responsibilities? Each family could as part of its annual contract agree to a statement of rights and responsibilities which goes beyond financial matters and discipline, and also describes expected levels of involvement in the class, in parent evenings, of membership in the School Association and participation in festivals, committees and Board. It would describe the rights and responsibilities of teachers in making all personnel and pedagogical decisions, of the Board in making financial and legal decisions, and of the School Association in having the task of providing a dialog forum for issues such as school schedules, tuition levels and financial assistance, in major development and capital projects, and perhaps in areas such as disciplinary procedures and conflict mediation. Equally the teachers would sign an annual agreement which would describe rights and responsibilities as professional colleagues. This includes being clear about principles of conduct between colleagues and between teachers and children.[15]

Agreements on rights and responsibilities between teachers/staff and parents can be supplemented by agreements with children in the high school in areas of dress code, substance abuse and disciplinary procedures, and the responsibility for monitoring such agreements can be given to a mixed faculty-student group.

The school is also part of a wider community—its local region and the community of Waldorf schools. What responsibility and what opportunity for service does the school have in its local community? Does it, should it, make its festivals available to the local community? Can it open its festivals to other communities? Is there the opportunity for civic engagement, for adult education, for local volunteer and service activities? It is good if a teacher is a member of the local Rotary club or of the volunteer ambulance corp. Is the school a member of the National Association of Independent Schools, and of the Association of Waldorf Schools of North America (AWSNA)? The mature Waldorf school can also reach out and mentor or provide assistance to new fledgling Waldorf schools in the region or support a public Waldorf-inspired initiative or a new Waldorf school in Africa, India or China. All of these activities of service give life and are part of the potential for flowering. For without this sharing and giving, an inner lassitude can set in so that we fail to recognize the many blessings which we have been given. Without service, a culture of mutual criticism, of gossip and cynicism can develop which becomes the antithesis of a healthy community life.

The inner side of this challenge of partnership is the question of how to foster true meetings between human beings. This is increasingly difficult in a time when our general culture promotes egotism and social fragmentation. As Rudolf Steiner notes repeatedly, we are increasingly isolated from each other as individuals, yet we long for community.[16] His answer to the question of a deeper meeting is that we need new social forms which help us to become conscious of our interdependence, and we need to develop a new practical social understanding which creates interest between people.[17] Waldorf school communities are new social forms, but they require a high level of social understanding and skill to work effectively. I sometimes think we have been given the legacy of new social forms but do not bring enough consciousness to the art of social creation, while conventional organizations have old forms but struggle mightily with a new social consciousness and skill to make them work. Servant leadership, group facilitation and communication skills, decision making by consensus, mediation processes, teamwork and a service orientation are attitudes and skills which the more conventional world is busily acquiring. We have much to learn in this regard so that we can develop a social art which facilitates the building of healthy communities. I believe a systematic learning in communication skills, nonviolent communication, group facilitation, conflict resolution and biography work, as well as in the arts of promoting healthy family life, is essential if Waldorf schools are to fulfill their promise of becoming seeds for a new society. The methods and approaches for acquiring such new social skills are readily available, but we need to overcome our prejudices and be willing to learn them.

Mature schools can consciously pick up this challenge and in so doing develop a spiritually-inspired social art that can facilitate the experience of community. Consciously sharing aspects of an individual's biography, having both a chairperson and a process coach who intervenes only in times of difficulty and helps in group review, practicing listening exercises and paraphrasing, having moments when teachers share what they are working with and struggling with in the classroom, and beginning and ending in a moment of silence are all methods with which we can work consciously. They will help to bring about more life and a deeper meeting between individuals.

Underlying the question of meeting skills is the question of how we deal with our difficulties and disagreements. Learning to name them, taking responsibility for our difficulties with each other, and all of us acquiring mediation and feedback skills are essential so that the unspoken judgments and untruths don't block our meeting. Individually we can picture our colleagues, note their strengths and weaknesses and remember when we have experienced something of their striving individuality. This activity and intention is beautifully expressed in Rudolf Steiner's reflections on faithfulness:

Faithfulness

Create for yourself a new, indomitable perception of faithfulness. What is usually called faithfulness passes so quickly. Let this be your faithfulness: You will experience

moments—fleeting moments—with the other person. The
human being will appear to you then as if filled, irradiated with
a spirit archetype. And then there may be—indeed, will be—
other moments, long periods of time when human beings are
darkened. But you will learn to say to yourself at such times:
"The Spirit makes me strong. I remember the archetype. I saw
it once. No illusion, no deception shall rob me of it." Always
struggle for the image that you saw. This struggle is faithfulness.
Striving thus for faithfulness, we shall be close to one another,
as if endowed with the protective power of angels.

– Rudolf Steiner

A Federated Organization: Mandates and Responsibility Groups

A third major challenge for a mature school is to find *new ways of
organizing the work of the school community.* The second phase of school
development is characterized by the differentiation and the gradual
professionalization of administration and decision-making forms. The
dangers of this phase over time are a gradual fragmentation and loss
of direction, characterized by long meetings, many committees and
poor coordination and communication. What was carried by the whole
faculty and by many committees can now be simplified, streamlined
and delegated to a few responsibility or mandate groups. If attention
has been paid to a qualitative renewal of the vision and mission of the
school, to re-enlivening the pedagogical principles of Waldorf education
and to a new understanding of mutual partnership, then the school
can look to principles of federation, of creating a smaller number of
responsibility groups with substantial autonomy and responsibility.
The Toronto Waldorf School and the Pine Hill Waldorf School (NH)
worked on this mode of organizing the work life of their schools for
some time in the 1990s. In the case of Toronto, the full faculty was the
mandating group to whom the mandate groups reported both their
issues and their decisions. In the case of Pine Hill, it was the College
of Teachers that was the main policymaking body, and in financial
matters, the Board of Trustees. Whereas the school before may have
had up to ten teacher committees and four or five Board committees,
now the school may have just three or four faculty mandate groups that
are empowered to make decisions on behalf of the whole, and one or

two Board mandate groups. A typical mandate structure for a Waldorf school might have the following kind of form:

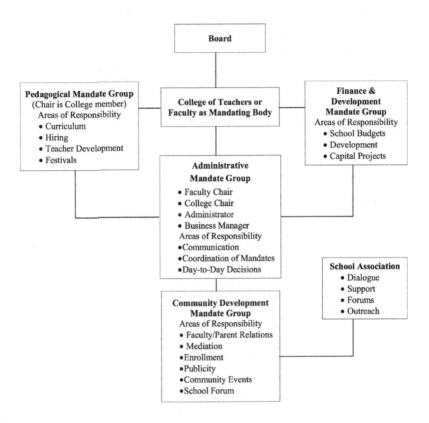

In creating a mandate organization, it is imperative to have a mandating body, which can be the full faculty, the College of Teachers or the Board. The mandate areas need to be clearly defined and then the best three to five people chosen to fulfill the tasks. Here the question should be what combination of people can best be responsible for this area of work on behalf of the whole. They need to have the trust of the faculty and/or Board and also be clear about their length of tenure and the policies which govern their area of work. The Pedagogical Mandate or responsibility group can only interview potential candidates for teaching positions if it knows what qualities are being looked for in teachers, what level of experience and training, what connection to anthroposophy. These are policy and value questions which the faculty or College of Teachers needs to have decided beforehand. Another required area of clarity is what decisions the mandate group can make for the whole and what not. Which decisions need to go to the full faculty or Board for input and which for decision?

Cornelis Pieterse has written an excellent overview of mandates in his short book, *Empowerment in Organizations—The Theory and Practice of a Mandate System.*[18] He rightly points to a distinction between constitutional mandates, like those of the Board of Trustees or the Teacher Council, as articulated in the Articles of Incorporation and the Bylaws of the school, and operational mandates, like those of the buildings and grounds group of the Board. In most cases the groups having a constitutional mandate are also the mandating bodies for the smaller operational mandate groups. In preparing and developing a mandate for a group, it is important to pay attention to the following elements:

- a short description of the mandate group's area of decision-making responsibility and areas for recommendation

- the reporting responsibilities of the mandate group (to College of Teachers, Board, Administration) and the frequency and manner of communication

- membership criteria, length of service, and selection process

- methods of clarifying the mandate or governing policies with the mandating group

- methods of soliciting input from members of the school community before making decisions

- review and evaluation of the mandate group's work

A critical aspect of a mandate organization is the facilitation and coordination of work. This can best be done by a mandate coordinating group which could consist of the Faculty Chairperson, the College Chairperson, and key administrative staff, perhaps the Business Manager, the Administrator and/or the development person.

The particular forms of a federated, mandate structure will vary from school to school, but the principle of the delegation of decision making to smaller groups based on the principles of competence and effectiveness is critical so that the College of Teachers, the faculty and the Board are free to do their essential work.

Another task connected to school forms at their mature phase of development is the task of penetrating the social and organizational structure of the school with the insights and ideals of spiritual science. Most Waldorf schools already work with some of these ideals, for example, in their collegial structures of decision making. Other steps would involve more intensive work with the fundamental social law of Rudolf Steiner in finding a new relation both to salaries and tuition income, or to deepening child study, or to permeating questions of inner development with more consciousness.

Many schools are moving away from needs-based salaries because it is too demanding, while others seek conventional solutions to financial and social issues. A deepening study of the social content of anthroposophy by the faculty and Board, and a more intensive sharing of the innovative practices of other Waldorf schools can become the inspiration for working with threefold principles in new ways.[19]

I believe it is only in true maturity and usually after the middle forties that individuals can give unselfishly to others. Similarly, it is in the phase of maturity, with a new commitment to their spiritual, pedagogical and social ideals, that Waldorf schools can become places where individuals and families can find the human, educational and spiritual nourishment so needed in our time.

A Conscious Ending?

If the pioneer stage can be likened to childhood, the differentiation phase to early and middle adulthood, and the integration phase to full maturity, what can be said about the death of an initiative? A convenient response is to say that schools die when they fail or are no longer needed. However, I feel that many institutions have not only become old, but also sclerotic, disposing of substantial resources, but no longer really serving human needs. If one pursues the human metaphor, perhaps institutions should live for only three generations or ninety years, if they are to serve the needs of the time. What would happen to cultural, social and economic creativity if institutions over ninety years old turned over their resources to new groups wishing to respond to similar needs in new ways? What a peaceful, on-going, creative revolution society would experience! Another approach is to renew an older institution by consciously turning over leadership to a younger generation, to allow a new body of teachers and administrators to continue the development of the school in new ways.

The Image of Development

What has been presented is a sketch of developmental patterns in a school's life. Frequently I am asked, "Can't a stage be missed?" The answer is no. Organizations have a life cycle moving from simple to more complex, from one central organizing principle to another. This means that true development is a discontinuous, yet irreversible process in time, moving from a stage of growth through differentiation to a higher stage of integration and passing through states of crisis which offer the impetus for development. This pattern is, I believe, true for all living forms—for the human being and for schools and other organizations.

However, it is possible for initiatives to move more or less rapidly through these phases. A school which starts with six grades and a kindergarten will face questions of differentiation much sooner than one which starts with one grade, adding a new grade each year. Furthermore, it is quite common for organizations to have different segments of the institution in different stages of development. A kindergarten and grade school may have entered the differentiation phase, while the school's new high school will be in its childhood pioneering period, and the two parts of the school will feel and function differently. This definitely needs to be appreciated by the many Waldorf schools now developing high schools after 25–30 years of existence.

In presenting this picture of school development, a number of complementary images have been alluded to. The image of birth, childhood, adulthood, and maturity is a metaphor which is quite clear. The qualities of intuitive, rational and conscious refer to the characteristic ways of approaching the world and of making decisions in the different phases in the life of the initiative. Another way of seeing this development process is to realize that the dialog with the spirit (identity), the dialog with people (relationships), and the dialog with the earth (resources) need to become ever more conscious in the school's life if the forces of decay and disintegration are not to become dominant over the course of time.

The description of school development outlined is both general and incomplete. Like all ideal-type descriptions, it cannot do justice to the rich texture of life in the Austin Waldorf School, or the City of Lakes Waldorf School in Minneapolis or the Emerson Waldorf School in Chapel Hill. Its purpose is rather to describe a landscape of possibilities, indicating paths to be pursued and pitfalls to be avoided so that we may become conscious co-creators of our Waldorf school communities.

Chapter II Reflections (individually or in small groups):

1) How and by whom was your Waldorf school started?

2) What are some of the typical themes or patterns of the school's biography (i.e., teacher-founded, rapid growth, well-funded, repeated major conflicts)?

3) Draw a picture of your school as a person. Is it a boy or a girl— large head, small feet? What does it say about your school?

4) What are some of the school's present strengths and weaknesses?

5) What phase of development is your school in?

6) If you had the opportunity, what are three things you would strengthen to aid the school in its development?

Endnotes

1. Allan Kaplan, *Development Practitioners and Social Process: Artists of the Invisible* (Pluto Press, London, XVCC 2002).

2. This essay is adapted from C. Schaefer & T. Voors, *Vision in Action: Working with the Soul and Spirit in Small Organizations,* 2nd Edition (Lindisfarne Press, Hudson, NY, 1996), pp. 27–58.

3. Both the picture of school development given and the various examples cited are based on many years of work by the author with Waldorf schools in the United States, Canada, the United Kingdom, Brazil, China and Mexico.

4. See L.E. Grenier, "Evolution and Revolution as Organizations Grow," *Harvard Business Review,* July-August, 1972.

5. A.C. Harwood, *The Recovery of Man in Childhood* (Rudolf Steiner Press, London, 1982).

6. This question list is adapted and modified from *Vision in Action,* pp. 81–83.

7. See Bernard Lievegoed, *The Developing Organization,* Tavisock Publications, 1973 (Celestial Arts, Berkeley, CA, 1979), pp. 55–61. Also, *Developing Communities* (Hawthorn Press, Stroud, UK, 1995).

8. See *Vision in Action,* pp. 163–177.

9. See *Vision in Action,* pp. 81–88, on giving mandates to committees.

10. See the essay by Ernst Lehrs, *Republican–Not Democratic,* available from the Association of Waldorf Schools of North America (Ghent, NY).

11. See the excellent booklet by Francis Gladstone, *Republican Academies,* for a detailed description of Steiner's intentions and his frustrations with collegial work in the first Waldorf school (Steiner Schools Fellowship, Forest Row, UK, 1997).

12. See Manfred Leist, *Parent Participation in the Life of a Waldorf School,* available from the Association of Waldorf Schools of North America (Ghent, NY).

13. The concept of these dialogs and of the threefold picture of the school is elaborated in *Vision in Action,* pp. 61–63.

14. Op. cit., Lievegoed, *Developing Communities,* p. 18.

15. See the excellent articles by Heinz Zimmerman, "What Conditions Are There for Taking Responsibility in an Independent Life of Culture?" and "What Is Happening in the Anthroposophical Society," 17.4 and 18.1, 1996, 1997 (Goetheanum, Switzerland).

16. Rudolf Steiner, *Social and Anti-Social Forces in the Human Being* (Mercury Press, Spring Valley, NY, 1984).

17. Rudolf Steiner, "How Can the Soul Needs of the Time Be Met?" (Zurich, October 10, 1946).

18. Cornelis Pieterse, *Empowerment in Organizations: The Theory and Practice of a Mandate System* (Rudolf Steiner College Press, Fair Oaks, CA, 2009), pp. 41–60.

19. See the excellent studies by Gary Lamb, *The Social Mission of Waldorf Education: Independent, Privately Funded and Accessible to All* (Association of Waldorf Schools of North America, Ghent, NY, 2004) and *Wellsprings of the Spirit* (AWSNA, 2006), for rich study material.

III

Self-Administration and Governance in Waldorf Schools

Seek the real practical life but seek it in a way that does not blind you to the spirit working in it. Seek the spirit but do not seek it out of spiritual egoism, from spiritual greed, but look for it because you want to apply it unselfishly in practical life, in the material world. Make use of the ancient principle: Spirit is never without matter, matter never without spirit.

— Rudolf Steiner

On April 23, 1919, Emil Molt, the owner of the Waldorf Astoria Cigarette Factory in Stuttgart, Germany, asked Rudolf Steiner to take on the planning and leadership of a school. Steiner agreed, and on September 15, the first Waldorf school opened with 256 children and eight grades. The school was founded in connection to Steiner's movement for the Threefold Social Order and was to be independent of state control and self-administered. "The school, therefore, will have its own administration run on a republican basis and will not be administered from above. We must not lean back and rest securely on the orders of a headmaster; we must be a republic of teachers and kindle in ourselves the strength that will enable us to do what we have to do with full responsibility."[1]

From these statements three principles emerge about self-administration: Schools must be free of state control as part of a free cultural life, teachers must be centrally involved in the running of the school and in decision making, and the school should be organized along republican principles in which teachers are equal but delegate specific responsibilities to individuals and committees. So Waldorf schools from the very beginning had a non-hierarchical social form in which individuals had to work on their relationships and experience the working of social and antisocial forces in themselves and in others.

In addition Steiner sought to integrate ideals from his work on broader social issues into the running of the first school. Salaries were not position- or job-based but needs-based, meaning that they reflected the prevailing sense of equity in the school community. Teachers with more dependents received higher salaries than those without, and neither degrees or length of service played into the financial support received. As the Stuttgart school was initially financed by the Waldorf Astoria factory and Emil Molt personally, tuitions were not charged to workers' children, although families from outside the factory paid what they could. It was hoped that as the Waldorf School Movement grew, local, regional and world school associations would develop in order to provide the financial support for an independent school movement. For Steiner it was not only a question of providing support for independent Waldorf schools but to demonstrate the principles of a free cultural life supported by the profits of economic life. "I am convinced that nothing is more important for the social development of humanity than the foundation of such a world association of schools which would then awaken a real sense for a free cultural life and spiritual life in the widest circle of people."[2] Such a World School Association was never created and Waldorf schools have become tuition-dependent (in the United States, Britain, France, China and Brazil) or partially publicly-funded (in Germany, Holland and the Scandinavian countries) or, as in the U.S., have become public charter schools, with better salaries but greater government regulation.

Principles of Self-Administration

The idea of Waldorf schools, and indeed of all schools, being free of state control is not difficult to grasp. The primary reason for this perspective is that governments, when they function well, are oriented towards equality and will therefore seek to impose uniform standards on all schools as well as to prescribe curriculum requirements. This severely limits the freedom and creativity of teachers and makes it difficult for a school to develop an education focused on the needs of the individual child. We have seen the negative consequences of "America 2000" and of the "No Child Left Behind Act" in the United States, as political and business elites impose their vision of education on teachers, children and parents, seldom involving teachers in the formulation of educational policy and goals.[3]

The issue was the same in Rudolf Steiner's time. Here he is speaking with the teachers in 1919: "Compromises are necessary as we have not yet reached the point where we can accomplish an absolutely free deed. The State will tell us how to teach and what results to aim for, and what the State prescribes will be bad. Its targets are the worst ones imaginable, yet it expects to get the best possible results. Today's politics work in the direction of regimentation, and it will go even further than this in its attempt to make people conform."[4]

Waldorf schools around the world are self-administered in the sense that there is no outside regional or national body that controls the running of a particular school. However, by self-administration Steiner primarily meant that teachers in a particular school should not only provide a quality education to the children but should also be centrally involved in decision making and administration. "The administration of education, from which all culture develops, must be turned over to the educators. Economic and political considerations should be entirely excluded from this administration. Each teacher should arrange his time so that he can also be an administrator in his field."[5] The rationale behind this view is that decisions about education and the school should flow out of a deep engagement with the children and their educational needs.

In understanding the principle of republican self-administration, it is helpful to return to an essay written by Ernst Lehrs, one of the early teachers in the first Waldorf school in Stuttgart. In *Republican–Not Democratic* (no reference to political parties), Lehrs notes that Steiner intended Waldorf schools to develop new social forms embodying three different and at times competing principles: aristocratic leadership, aristocratic meaning "the best"; delegated responsibilities to groups and individuals by the *res publica*, the common body of teachers; and democratic selection of such individuals and groups based on competence and skill. Teachers exercised their free initiative (aristocratic leadership), both in the classroom and in carrying out their chosen and delegated administrative roles. They were also part of a republic of teachers who made all important pedagogical and administrative decisions together democratically.[6] As Francis Gladstone notes in *Republican Academies*, a short study providing an excellent description of the principles and practice of self-administration in the first Waldorf school, "The merit of the republican approach is that it secures individual freedom, a necessary condition for creative work. Its danger is that the members of the republic fail to use that freedom to work together towards a common end. And when the give and take of free cooperation is absent, social harmony evaporates and unity is lost."[7] Then as now the two great dangers of republican self-administration in Waldorf schools are that individuals and groups who have been given specific mandates or responsibilities are not allowed to do their job, being interfered with or criticized by the full faculty or Board, and the opposite, that those chosen for positions of responsibility or who volunteer for them become a *de facto* oligarchy, building up their power at the expense of the teacher circle.[8] These issues are discussed in some length in chapters II and IV.

We should not wonder that many teachers and parents today struggle with understanding how their Waldorf school works, how leadership, governance and decision making are exercised. Even in Steiner's time the struggle to blend the values of individual freedom and creativity, the selection of individuals and groups based on competence, and the functioning of a teacher republic working with democratic principles, was messy.[9]

A Historical Perspective:

While the Rudolf Steiner School in New York was founded in 1928, the great majority of Waldorf schools in the U.S. were created after World War II and in particular in the 1960s, 1970s and 1980s. The individuals who played a significant role in founding many of these schools were Frances Edmunds, Henry Barnes, Werner Glas and René Querido, all Waldorf educators and lecturers who traveled the country extensively supporting new school groups. Each of them had their formative Waldorf experience in English Waldorf schools: Henry Barnes, Frances Edmunds and René Querido at Michael Hall School in Forest Row, and Werner Glas at Wynstones and Edinburgh. English law being similar to American law meant that schools in both countries were non-profit organizations or charitable trusts, with a Board of Directors or Trustees that was legally responsible for the school in the eyes of the state. In the English and later in the American Waldorf schools, this meant that teachers and some parents and friends of the school were the directors of the school, with a faculty circle making most important pedagogical, administrative and financial decisions. Early Waldorf schools in both England and the United States were indeed faculty-run schools with limited administration and Boards which existed mainly to support the teachers in their work.

It was only from the late 1970s on that well-established Waldorf schools grew in size and complexity and needed larger administrative staffs and Boards which had greater financial, legal and fundraising expertise. It was then in the 1980s and 1990s that some Waldorf schools developed a picture of school governance and decision making which was based on a conception of partnership between a strong faculty or College of Teachers and a strong Board, consisting mainly of parents, a Board which saw itself as responsible for the financial health of the school as well as for the competence and professionalism of the school's administration.

I remember attending the early "Healthy Waldorf School" conferences sponsored by AWSNA and being struck by the emergence of this different conception of the Board's role. The argument which began to emerge at these meetings and in other conversations was that the parent body made the school possible through sending their children and providing the financial resources for it to work. As some members of the parent community had the requisite legal, financial and fundraising skills needed by the school, should not members of the parent body form the majority of the Board and work to provide the physical, financial and administrative resources to support the teachers in their work? This perspective made sense to increasing numbers of parents and teachers so that more Waldorf schools began to work with partnership forms of governance in which the teachers carried all pedagogical and hiring responsibility and the Board, including teacher representatives, the legal and financial responsibility. In this approach the administration was seen as serving both the faculty and the Board, with some administrative functions having more a pedagogical quality, such as Faculty or College Chair and others, such as Finance and Development, being closer to central Board responsibilities.

I would say that a third approach to Waldorf school governance has emerged since the turn of the century, in particular based on the work of John Carver who, looking at the legal responsibilities of a Board, refined its leadership role in regard to the mission, values, policies and guidance of an institution.[10] Schools such as the Seattle Waldorf School and the Vancouver Waldorf School have worked with this approach and have each chosen to have a school director, responsible to both Board and faculty. While this is clearly a departure from Steiner's original intention, it is an understandable development given the complexity of mature Waldorf schools and the desire for clarity and accountability.

Each of these three approaches to Waldorf school governance has its rationale and virtues. There are successful Waldorf schools working with each approach as well as with combinations of these structures as each school rightly is engaged in finding those forms and processes which most effectively meet its present needs.

Waldorf School Forms: Roles and Responsibilities

In all schools, teachers, parents and administrative staff are there to serve the needs of the growing and developing child. In developed Waldorf schools there are typically three main decision-making groups and eight main group meetings, not counting committees and task groups. The three main decision-making groups are the faculty (Faculty Council) and/or College of Teachers, the Board of Trustees and an Executive Committee or Leadership Group. In some Waldorf schools the full faculty is the main decision-making body on all pedagogical and personnel questions (the Toronto Waldorf School worked this way for many years), and in others it is the College of Teachers. Whether a Faculty Council or a College of Teachers, the main responsibilities of the faculty body include:

- Deepening the understanding and commitment of the teachers to Waldorf education through pedagogical and child study as a way of inspiring the teaching and each other.

- Assuring educational excellence through the hiring, mentoring, evaluation and dismissal of teachers and staff and developing the appropriate policies and processes for this to take place.

- Carrying the festival life of the school.

- Overseeing the administrative life and the scheduling of school activities.

- Understanding and developing the school budget together with the Board finance committee and the school's finance department.

- Selecting delegates or representatives to sit on the Board of Trustees and other groups and committees.

- Creating mandates and establishing committees to carry out the work of the faculty, such as a personnel committee or a festival committee.

- Carrying a sense for the whole life of the school and being committed to learning and development for the school through workdays, review of meetings and a sensing of the school community's health.

For Steiner the teacher's meeting was the heart and soul of the school's life.

> We have our Teacher's Meeting in the Waldorf school which is the heart and soul of the whole teaching. In these meetings, each teacher speaks of what he himself has learned in his class and from all the children in it, so that each one learns from the other. No school is really alive where this is not the most important thing, this regular meeting of teachers.[11]

Realizing this imagination of a creative, inquiring academy of teachers sharing their insights is critical to the health of Waldorf education. To keep even a semblance of this dream alive in today's world requires great vigilance in not letting business absorb all the time and energy of the faculty. Good planning, a clear agenda, and a conscious and disciplined Faculty Chair, as well as the ongoing delegation of tasks to committees and mandate groups are essential conditions for allowing this space for teacher creativity and sharing.

In many developed Waldorf schools the full faculty meeting, including the administrative staff, is more an all-school meeting, a space for artistic work, study, and announcements and scheduling, whereas decisions are made either by a College or Council of Teachers or in what are often called the section meetings: Early Childhood, Grades Faculty and High School Faculty. The College of Teachers, which exists in many Waldorf schools, is a body of faculty members and staff who have made a commitment to the particular school, to Waldorf pedagogy and to the path of inner development in anthroposophy. They see themselves as being spiritually responsible for the school and its well being. Usually the College of Teachers also works with the teacher's imagination and verse which Rudolf Steiner gave to the teachers of the first Waldorf school. Information on the forming of a College of Teachers can be acquired from the Association of Waldorf Schools of North America (AWSNA) and the Pedagogical Section of the School of Spiritual Science of the General Anthroposophical Society.[12]

The second important decision-making group in Waldorf schools is the Board of Trustees or Directors. The Board typically carries the following responsibilities:

- Seeing that the mission and purpose of the school is being realized.

- Assuring the financial health of the school through good financial policies and administration as well as fostering a robust development (fundraising) effort.

- Seeing that all local, regional and national legal requirements are being met.

- Together with the faculty, choosing quality administrative staff to serve the school.

- Developing and maintaining the physical plant of the school which includes responsibility for the Capital Campaigns conducted by the school.

- Initiating and coordinating Long Term or Strategic Planning in the school.

Most Waldorf school Boards consist of nine to twelve people, with a majority of parents and friends of the school and usually from two to four teacher representatives selected by the faculty or the College of Teachers. Boards are usually self-perpetuating with a nominating committee selecting new candidates based on their experience and expertise. Typically Board terms are from two to three years, renewable once or twice thus assuring some turnover in Board membership. In some schools the Chair of the Parent Association or a representative of the Parent Association is elected to the Board.

Typically standing Board committees include Finance, Development, Buildings and Grounds, Capital Campaign, and Long Term or Strategic Planning. Committee membership is not limited to Board members, as both faculty and parents may be asked to join, thus familiarizing them with Board work and preparing them for possible future Board membership.

A third important decision-making group in many Waldorf schools is the Executive Committee or Leadership Group which meets weekly to make operating decisions on behalf of the school. Typically this committee or group consists of the lead Administrator, the Faculty Chair, the College Chair and sometimes the head of the Finance Department. Such a group functions somewhat like a collective school head or principal and serves to integrate the interests of faculty, Board and administration. It can function well as long as it communicates effectively with these three bodies, has their trust and confidence and is able to draw upon a well-developed body of policies for guidance in decisions.

In addition to these decision-making groups, there are a number of other important meetings and groups working in the school. These include the section meetings of Early Childhood, Grade and High School Faculty, the weekly administrative staff meeting and the Parent Teacher Association. The Parent-Teacher or Parent Association is an important part of the school but is often not well understood by either faculty or parents. In my experience it works most effectively when it sees its role as primarily building and strengthening the whole school community, meaning that it supports the teachers through providing class parents who assist the class teachers, communicating issues of parent concern to the faculty, and conducting all-school meetings or forums on topics as diverse as next year's budget and the school's media policy. It should also play a role in adult education by requesting courses, lectures and seminars on topics of general interest to Waldorf school parents. Typically it will also be involved in the Winter Fair and other school benefits. However the Board or Development Committee needs to be careful not to turn the Parent Association into a fundraising arm, as this can undermine its essential communicating and community-building role. In some schools the Parent Association will also have a role in the orientation of new parents and in developing and implementing a parent-teacher dispute resolution process.

In many Waldorf schools the Parent Association with its chair or co-chairs will be very active for a few years and then will almost disappear as the volunteer energy of a few energetic mothers wanes. This is to be expected as only a quarter to a third of parents are actively interested in understanding and supporting the school through volunteering their time and talents. As the need for this energy and commitment is great, from serving on Board committees to class parent duties, not too mention the Winter Fair and other benefit activities, it is easy to see that after three to four years of intensive involvement activity decreases. Then in a few years new parents will seize the opportunity to make a difference in the life of a school and again activate the work of the PTA.

Threefold Perspectives

We have noted previously that for a human being to be healthy we need a spiritual purpose and sense of direction, we need friends, family and meaningful relationships and we need to attend to our physical health and well-being. I once heard a medical doctor say that he asked his patients three questions: Are you on a path of inner development? Do you love someone? Do you like your work? If they could answer each of these questions positively, he felt that they were likely to be well. In hearing him speak, I realized that I ask my organizational clients a similar set of questions: How is your dialog with the spirit, with the mission values and central purpose of your organization, and how do you keep this dialog alive? What are the qualities of the dialog between people, the nature of the relationships between the teachers, parents, children and administrative staff, and how do you seek to strengthen these relationships? Thirdly, what is the quality of the dialog with the earth, with finances, buildings and grounds, with the material well-being of your school? I found that when teachers did not understand or agree on the central aspects of Waldorf education and the profound and rich image of child development at the heart of the curriculum, then relationships in the school suffered since people could not trust others to be striving in the same direction, working toward the same star. Then if trust was lacking between people, work arrangements, committee assignments and delegation did not function, undermining the effective working of the school. If we have a body, soul and spirit, then all social creations—families, groups and institutions—also do, and it becomes our task as parents, teachers and staff to see that the dialogs in these three domains are as alive and healthy as possible.

We can also see that the three dialogs in the school are related to the three essential qualities of social life described by Rudolf Steiner in *Toward Social Renewal*, the book in which he first described the characteristics of the Threefold Social Order.[13] For there to be a healthy spiritual life in society and in a Waldorf school, individuals need to experience freedom in their teaching and in the forming of insights, values and judgments. Yet a Waldorf school (and indeed any community) also needs a common vision, an agreement on the central nature of Waldorf education, on the pedagogy and the picture of child development. So *freedom* as a principle for the *dialog with spirit* needs to be balanced by common vision and striving. When I have worked with Waldorf schools in which teachers had very different visions of what Waldorf education was, then inevitably relationships suffered and work agreements broke down. In these situations no amount of work on governance structures or on relationships will resolve the underlying disunity of purpose.

The *dialog between people* rests on mutual respect, seeing the other as an equal human being. This is the realm of *equality*, of human rights and responsibilities. In Waldorf schools this dialog is fostered through consensus decision making, the exercise of democratic rights and the many groups and committees which make up the life of the school. It also comes to expression in clear agreements, ranging from employment contracts, tuition agreements, dress codes, media policies and disciplinary procedures. In Western societies there is a pronounced focus on rights with much less attention paid to responsibilities. This is also true of Waldorf schools. Yet for schools to function well, the rights of the individual need to be balanced by our responsibilities and obligations to each other and to the school. It is not acceptable for a teacher to decide not to attend faculty meetings or to avoid committee assignments, or for a parent not to attend class evenings or to withhold tuition payments because of some grievance with the school. The new community forms of Waldorf schools can easily be exploited by individuals seeking power or not wishing the school well, so that we need the balancing protection of clear agreements which spell out expectations in a host of areas including: committee mandates, Board membership, selection and responsibilities, employee contracts, grievance and disciplinary procedures and financial contracts. Only in this way can both rights and responsibilities be protected and a healthy rights life fostered based on equality and mutual understanding.

The *dialog with the earth* is concerned with the school's work life, its finances and relationships with the buildings and campus of the school. In this realm of economic life Steiner refers to brotherhood and sisterhood or *fraternity* as the essential qualities for societies to foster. In schools this dialog comes to expression in a concern with competence and service in the administration and the selection of individuals for tasks and responsibilities, in the clarity and transparency of the school's finances and the effort to make the education affordable to as many families as possible, and in the concern for the beauty and cleanliness of buildings and grounds.

All the partners of the Waldorf school community are involved in all three dialogs, for example in the festival life which seeks to enliven the dialog with the spirit, or in all-school meetings and the many groups and committees which make up the dialog between people in the school, or in the financial life of the school which affects everyone. However in exploring the threefold character of Waldorf schools in the Waldorf School Administration and Community Development Program at Sunbridge College over many years, we also came to see three distinct cultures in the school's life, each strongly associated with one of the three dialogs.

The first is the *teacher* or the *pedagogical culture* of the school. This culture is more strongly focused on the ideals of truth, beauty and goodness, on the teacher as the guardian and facilitator of the child's healthy incarnation and development. The teacher culture and its formal institutional expression in the College of Teachers or the weekly faculty meeting is primarily concerned with fostering the dialog with *spirit*, with the spirit of the child, the spirit of the class and the spirit of the school. It is fostered through the process of inner spiritual development the teacher engages in, through the teacher meditation and through the inspiration and creativity of the teaching process.

The dialog with the *earth* is strongly connected to the central responsibilities of *the Board and the parent community*. Their task is to help incarnate the school, to provide the human and financial resources to help the school develop its physical home and its financial base. Here the central values are service and competence so that the abundant resources of the parent community can flow into the school and provide a healthy basis for the educational process. Professionalism, performance orientation, efficient use of resources, action learning, capacity development and competent service are the watchwords of this service culture which is strongly carried by the Board and the parent community.

The dialog between *people*, of course, involves the *whole school community*. It is the *meeting culture* so central and at times so frustrating in the life of Waldorf schools. Here interest in the other, the art of conversation, true meetings, recognizing that we are destiny partners on the road of mutual development are important values to practice, and developing social sensitivity, effective communication and group skills capacities to acquire. The meeting culture and fostering clarity in the institutional process are strongly carried by the school's administration which exists to serve and balance the educational work of teachers and the Board's and parents' role in providing the financial and physical basis of the education.

These reflections on threefold perspectives in the life of a Waldorf school are summarized in the following chart:

The Dialog with Spirit—
    Freedom and Common Vision— Teacher Culture
                      Aristocratic
The Dialog between People—
    Equality (Rights and Responsibilities)—Meeting Culture
                      Democratic
The Dialog with the Earth—
    Fraternity (Competence and Service)—Service Culture
                      Republican

At the beginning of this essay, Ernst Lehr's comments on aristocratic, democratic and republican leadership in the first Waldorf school were described and the difficulty of combining these qualities noted. This is also visible when comparing the three cultures and their shadow sides. For the teacher culture the shadow side is often: "We know Waldorf education so you can't possibly understand the rationale for our decision." For the meeting culture it is: "I thought we are an alternative institution in which all things are decided democratically and we haven't had an adequate process with this decision." For the service culture the call can be: "Why are we so inefficient, why so many meetings? If only we had effective managerial leadership and a clear cost benefit analysis of this decision." The one-sided dangers of spiritual arrogance, of excessive democratic process and of managerial economic efficiency are clear to anyone who has spent time working in a Waldorf school. Unless parents, teachers and staff are all committed to reflection and self-development, the new community partnership forms of Waldorf schools can easily be subverted and the social impulse of Waldorf eduction lost.

The three, balancing cultures form the basis of the three-pillar model of Waldorf school governance described by Robert Schiappacasse in *Administrative Explorations.*[14] It is a visual portrayal of a set of threefold principles, values and structures which can help each school to reflect on its governance and administrative forms and determine those changes which can serve the school's further development.

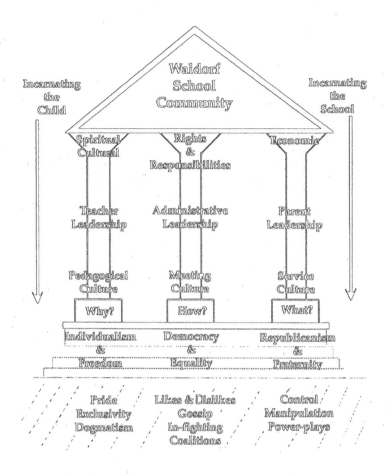

Incarnating the Child

Incarnating the School

Waldorf School Community

Spiritual Cultural	Rights & Responsibilities	Economic
Teacher Leadership	Administrative Leadership	Parent Leadership
Pedagogical Culture	Meeting Culture	Service Culture
Why?	How?	What?
Individualism & Freedom	Democracy Equality	Republicanism & Fraternity
Pride Exclusivity Dogmatism	Likes & Dislikes Gossip In-fighting Coalitions	Control Manipulation Power-plays

What Teachers, Parents and Administrators Want

It is important to recognize that the complex threefold nature of Waldorf school governance may well meet the needs of Waldorf school teachers, parents, administrators and children more effectively than either public schools with their politically determined top heavy administration or the headmaster and Board-run model of most private schools. In many conversations with both Waldorf and public school teachers, I have found that most teachers want to be able to meet the children in a free and creative manner through offering a curriculum that responds to the children's needs for an age-appropriate, stimulating and holistic education. Out of their experience in eduction and their love of children, they want a level of freedom in determining the content of their lessons and a say in choosing their colleagues.

Administrators, if they have not been brainwashed by corporate models of education, want to support and nurture the educational process and be perceived as equal partners by teachers and parents in their work of carrying out the myriad administrative tasks required for the efficient running of a successful school. In most cases they do not wish to be the bosses of teachers, recognizing the need for substantial autonomy in the classroom.

Children want to be seen by the teachers for the individuals that they are and to be enthused by learning. I recently did a school audit at a young Waldorf school and in interviewing parents was frequently told that their children hated being sick because they missed their classmates and teachers. It was a clear statement of a Waldorf school's meeting its children's needs successfully.

For parents their children are precious, and in sending them to a particular school they hope against hope that their children will be seen, loved, encouraged and educated to reach their potential. They also want to be able to understand the education their child is receiving and to be able to support it financially and with their time, energy and knowledge.

The friends, alumni, former parents and supporters of Waldorf education also wish to have the possibility of helping, of getting involved with their time, energy and resources. I remember an elderly women who had not met Waldorf education and anthroposophy when her children were growing up but who nevertheless spent countless hours on the Board of a newly-established Waldorf school in her community.

If this picture of the learning partnership is true, then the non-hierarchical complex governance and administrative forms of Waldorf schools go a long way toward meeting the central aspirations of teachers, parents, administrators and children. While at times messy, these school forms are lively, engaging and challenging and allow all of us to experience the joys and struggles of building a creative educational community together.[15]

The Developing Administration

In the early years of a Waldorf school, administrative work is a *d hoc* and volunteer based. Parents take turns answering the phones during class hours, function as receptionists, gardeners and file clerks and even do the simple accounting required to keep the books in order. While a bit chaotic, it is energizing to work toward realizing the dream of establishing a school. A few years later, with a nursery, kindergarten and one or two grades, one of the volunteers with an interest in administration joins the school on a part-time or full-time basis in administration, and year by year the administration grows.

Generally more mature Waldorf schools have one administrative staff person for every 35 to 40 children enrolled. The challenge for the Board and the faculty is to gradually help the administration grow from a collection of volunteers with a mixed assortment of skills to a more professional administration. Typically the first two functions which become paid are the receptionist and bookkeeper. A young and growing Waldorf school which I worked with recently has three Parent-Tot programs, two Nursery Groups and two Kindergarten Groups as well as six grades. Its total enrollment is over 200 children and it has the following administrative positions:

Director of Administration: A full-time position to oversee all administrative work, chair the administrative staff meeting and chair the school's Leadership Group. Accountable to Board and faculty.

Enrollment Director: A full-time position to handle all aspects of admissions, from advertising to interviewing, admissions and enrollment contracts. Works with a part-time assistant.

Finance Director: Responsible for budgeting, bookkeeping, financial planning, capital budgets and collections. With one full-time assistant and one bookkeeper.

Communications Coordinator: A part-time position to handle all written and e-mail communication within the school and to coordinate scheduling work.

Receptionist and Security: A part-time position responsible for answering phones and keeping an eye on front door security.

Maintenance and Cleaning: Two part-time positions to deal with repairs and ongoing cleaning in the building.

In addition to these 7.5 positions in administration, the school has a faculty chair for the grade school and an early childhood education chair. While these positions are now filled by individuals with full-time teaching loads, it is anticipated that their teaching loads will be reduced so that they can more adequately carry out their important pedagogical administrative work.

The school described does not yet have a development coordinator or director as the bulk of fundraising work is still done by the Board of Trustees. This is typical of younger Waldorf schools, and it can be expected that in the coming years, the school will add one to two people in development and possibly a part-time coordinator of volunteers.

Fully-developed Waldorf schools will also have at least four positions in pedagogical administration: an Early Childhood Chair, a Grade School Faculty Chair, a College of Teachers Chair and a High School Coordinator or Chair. The development of pedagogical or faculty administrative work has happened gradually over the last decades so that it is clear that the administration of most Waldorf schools has two sides: a faculty administration directly serving and responsible to the teachers, and a financial, enrollment and development administration more responsible to the Board of Trustees. It is however important to recognize that both types of administration need to be able to work together well and to have the trust and confidence of both faculty and Board.

There are two significant dangers in hiring for administrative positions in Waldorf schools. The first is to hire people with administrative experience and expertise from the non-profit or business world but with no experience or understanding of Waldorf education. The culture of Waldorf schools is unique and without a relationship to Waldorf education or anthroposophy, it is difficult for capable administrators to find their way into the language, practices and assumptions which permeate our culture. The many meetings, the lack of hierarchy and sometimes the lack of clarity and accountability can drive people used to other organizational cultures crazy. The other danger is to assume that anyone can do administrative work and to hire a trained Waldorf teacher who is tired of the classroom to fill an administrative job. This also seldom works unless the person in question enjoys administrative work, establishing the order and clear processes involved in carrying out the myriad tasks which need to be done to support the education. So it is best to find people who understand and love Waldorf education and who also have experience and talent in carrying out specific administrative tasks. Increasingly such people exist in the talented parent body of many Waldorf schools.

As the need for clarity is critical for successful administrative work in schools, it is important to have clear job descriptions for the school's administration. These can be requested from mature Waldorf schools who have had many years to develop clear descriptions or from ASWNA.

Because Waldorf teachers are used to functioning as equals in the faculty circle, it is sometimes thought that this should also be the case among administrative staff. In my experience this is seldom effective, as people will tend do that part of the job they like unless they are clearly accountable to someone. A well-developed school should consider having a director of administration to oversee the 10 to 12 people involved in the important work of having an efficient and well-running administration.

Clarity, Social Skills and Self-Development

When asked to speak about the principles and practices of Waldorf school governance and administration in Waldorf school communities, I tend to stress the need for clarity, for articulating the underlying principles of governance and decision making in the school before moving to a description of the main tasks, membership, decision-making responsibility and mutual accountability of each group. Newer parents often want to know who is in charge. The best answer is to say we all are and then to inquire which area of the school's life is being referred to. Many Waldorf school Parent Handbooks have good descriptions of self-administration and school governance, but it is always good to remind everyone how the school runs and who makes what decisions. In the end, however, it is what happens in the classroom that is paramount. If children are happy, then parents are happy. If, however, things are not going well in a number of classes, then the unease spreads to other areas of the school's life as parents seek to understand what is wrong, often looking at leadership and administration for answers to the problem of inadequate teaching.

It is clear that Waldorf schools are a dialog culture, with their many committees, meetings and groups. Possessing good social and group facilitation skills is critical for individuals in leadership and chair positions in the school. It makes a world of difference if a meeting is chaired well, and this is a skill which can be learned. The new social forms of Waldorf schools require a higher form of social insight and skill than more traditional organizations with their command and control structures.

New social and community forms can work only if all adult members of the school community are reflective and engaged in a process of self-transformation and development. The reason for this is that Waldorf schools foster a deeper meeting between adults than most other kinds of institutions, and deeper meetings mean more conflict. Unless we are capable of self-reflection and understand the ways in which others push our buttons, then Waldorf schools will resemble present-day American politics and will be unable to serve the children's needs well. This does not mean that all adults should become students of anthroposophy, but it does mean that Waldorf schools should promote self-reflection, common learning, and self-transformation through spiritual and meditative work.

Endnotes

1. Rudolf Steiner, *Education as Art* (Blauvelt, NY, Garber Publications, 1970), pp. 74–75. I am indebted to Gary Lamb for many useful insights and quotes from Rudolf Steiner on educational freedom. In particular see Gary Lamb, *The Social Mission of Waldorf Education: Independent, Privately Funded and Accessible to All* (Association of Waldorf Schools of North America, Ghent, NY, 2004).

2. Op. cit., Lamb, p. 33.

3. Ibid., pp. 71–83 in particular.

4. Rudolf Steiner, *Conferences with the Teachers of the Waldorf School in Stuttgart*, Vol.1 (Steiner Schools Fellowship, Forest Row, England, 1986), p. 34.

5. Op. cit., Lamb, p. 40.

6. Ernst Lehrs, *Republican–Not Democratic* (AWSNA Publications, Great Barrington, MA, 1987), pp. 1–7.

7. Gladstone, Francis. *Republican Academies: Rudolf Steiner on Self-Management, Experiential Study and Self-Education in the Life of a College of Teachers* (Forest Row, England, Steiner Schools Fellowship, 1997), p. 17.

8. Op. cit., Lehrs, pp. 3–7.

9. Op. cit., Gladstone, pp. 13–22.

10. John Carver, *Boards That Make a Difference: A New Design for Leadership in Nonprofit and Public Organizations* (San Francisco, CA, Jossey-Bass, 1997), in particular pp. 1–74.

11. Rudolf Steiner, *The Spiritual Ground of Education* (Blauvelt, NY, Garber Publications, 1987), pp. 93–94.

12. Contact ASWNA at info@awsna.org, as well as the pedagogical section representatives in North America.

13. Rudolf Steiner, *Toward Social Renewal* (SteinerBooks, Great Barrington, MA, 1987).

14. Robert Schiappacasse, "Three Pillars of Healthy Waldorf Communities," in *Administrative Explorations*, David Mitchell and David Alsop, eds., (AWSNA, Fair Oaks, CA, 2000), pp. 3–11. The diagram is also from this article and was developed with faculty and students at the Waldorf School Administration and Community Development Program.

15. Christopher Schaefer, "Enhancing the Learning Partnership through New School Forms: The Waldorf Experience," in *Holistic Education Review*, Vol. 9, No. 2 (Brandon, VT, 1996), pp. 40–48.

IV

Working Together in Groups and Communities

*All men are caught in an inescapable network of mutuality, tied in
a single garment of destiny. Whatever affects one directly affects all
indirectly. I can never be what I ought to be until you are what you
ought to be. And you can never be what you ought to be until I am
what I ought to be.*

– Martin Luther King

Conversation

We take a mystery of life for granted, the mystery of conversation.
Reflect on how an impression in your consciousness—"the beauty of
a San Francisco spring morning with the fog blowing off the Bay"—
is translated into concepts and then into audible speech, involving
all the complex muscles of the throat and mouth. Your friend hears
these words through the membrane of the ear and understands them,
internalizes your thought and then speaks. One aspect of the mystery
is how we are able to turn consciousness, the non-sensory, into audible
speech and visible gesture. Another is how the other is able to take the
sounds expressed and make sense of them. A third is how in dialog, in
conversation between two or more individuals, something new, an idea,
meaning or decision arises.

In conversation, we can recognize three parties: I, you and that
which arises between us. We can also become aware of three central
processes: of speaking, of turning ideas into audible speech and visible
gesture; of listening, taking the others meaning into oneself; and third,
of understanding, individually and together.[1] Each process requires
consciousness and attention. The more focused our consciousness, the
better the result.

For speaking, we can ask ourselves: What are the essential elements I want to communicate? What examples and images will make it intelligible to the other? What words or images will make sense to her or him? Can I be brief so the other doesn't get lost?

In listening, we can ask: Can I be still? Can I focus on the thought, words, gestures of the other? Can I not react until they are finished? Can I really be present with loving interest? Can I ask questions for clarification before I respond?

For understanding, we can reflect on: Is it clear for me? Am I being understood? Can I see where there are similarities and differences in how we see the question? Can I bring an attitude of mutuality, of joint creation to the conversation and notice that which is new?

Types of Groups in Relation to Dominant Activities

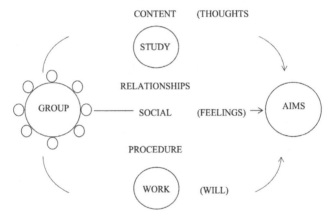

In the process of speaking, listening and understanding we are externalizing our soul being, we are sharing who we are. This involves more than words and ideas; it includes our feelings and intentions. So we are creating a kind of soul music in conversation, the melody of our thoughts and ideas, the feeling content of harmonies, disharmonies, crescendos and pianissimos and the rhythm and beat of our willed intention. Our ideas are usually most conscious, our likes, dislikes and feelings less so, and our intentions least conscious.

The more we are able to put our full being, our whole soul at the disposal of the present moment without preconceptions and a lot of agendas, the more we are capable of being social artists, allowing the magic of conversation to work between us.[2] I used to meet frequently with a friend over lunch in order to share what was happening in our lives and to talk about our process of inner development. The topics ranged from work, our children and marriages to questions of meditation. He listened so well and was so present that the conversation was always alive, spontaneous and enriching.

If we pay attention to what happens to our consciousness in conversation, we can notice an ebb and flow between being awake to ourselves, to our ideas and feelings when we are speaking and then, in listening, being more awake to others and less conscious of ourselves. In speaking we are in ourselves, busy with the task of articulating our thoughts, feelings and intentions, and in listening we leave our own soul space and enter into that of the other. For most of us true listening is infinitely more difficult and tiring than speaking, for it asks us to silence our inner chatter and attend to someone else.

Rudolf Steiner describes a meeting, a conversation between two individuals as the archetypal social phenomenon, suggesting that it is the essential building block of community, of society.[3] We are always part of a language community, whether it be English, Spanish, Chinese, Yoruba or Balinese, and through our cultural upbringing we share a universe of meaning. Police stations are not coffee shops, nor schools dry-cleaners; at least that is not their intention. Within the context of language and meaning we engage in acts of social creation—buying a shirt, renting a car, planning a parent evening or starting a school. We carry out these acts by and through dialog. By attending to this dialog, to conversation in all its forms, we can learn more about that mysterious process of social creation which results when two or more human beings meet together.[4]

Different Types of Groups

Conversations happen in structured and unstructured group settings: refreshments after a school festival, the finance committee meeting or a study group on Waldorf education. It is important to know what kind of a group we are attending and to be clear about mutual expectations. It doesn't do for me to explore my interests in planetary cycles and the phases of human development in the finance committee meeting or for you to insist on a set agenda and clear decision by consensus in a study group.

Study groups share written or spoken material, exploring themes of mutual interest: 19th century novels, birds of the northwest or the challenge of raising children in the 21st century. Participants come together mainly to enrich each other's insight and experience, not with the intention of agreeing on some point or doing a common task. Social groups are mutual support groups; they are there to understand, enjoy and support each other, whether in the form of a 12-step program or through a weekly game of cards between friends. The purpose is the meeting and the sharing between people. Work groups on the other hand have discrete tasks external to the group: planning the Christmas fair, preparing next year's budget or evaluating candidates for next year's first grade.

While all groups have a content (study) element, a social relational element and a task (work) dimension, they tend to be focused on one area more than the others.[5]

In any group it is important to achieve mutual clarity on the purpose of the group, its particular aims and the format and style of the meeting. Discussing the purpose, aims and responsibilities of groups avoids countless problems later on because it harmonizes expectations.

The Cycle of Mutual Learning

All too often learning in groups happens outside of the meeting— in a hallway between friends or on the way home in the car. "That was a great meeting! How come it was so dead?" "Carl continued to monopolize. Why won't he learn?" "We wasted a lot of time, didn't we?" The learning is not shared by everyone and often not by those we wish would change. Worst of all, by informally evaluating, we don't take responsibility for the success or failure of the meeting, often feeling it's the responsibility of the chairperson or the convener. So it is good to follow a basic principle with all groups, but in particular with work groups: Plan together first, then have the meeting and then briefly review together in the group.

On planning

Make sure the room is properly set up and everyone is present. Then begin with a moment of silence or a verse to center consciousness. Then you can check: What is our agenda? Which points are for discussion, which for decision? Can we allocate time according to the importance of the topics? Do we have all the relevant information for each topic under discussion? Who will chair the meeting? Who will take notes?

In the meeting

During the meeting make sure that all the group members have the opportunity to speak and be listened to by everyone and that there is a reasonable balance between speaking and listening. Take time for decisions especially if you are working by consensus.

In review

Then allow five or ten minutes to review the results and process of the meeting. Some questions to consider are:

Mood: How was the mood of the meeting? Where were the high and low points and why? Were there tensions and how were they worked with?

Procedure: Were we clear about the agenda and the aims of the meeting? Did we accomplish what we set out to do? Where did we get lost? How was the decision-making process? What did we do well, what less well? Did we use our time efficiently?

Speaking and listening: Were people able to speak? Did contributions build on each other? How was the listening? How was participation and engagement? Did sub-groups dominate?

Leadership roles: How was the chairing? Was there help with the process from others? Who played what informal roles?

Learning: What are two things that we could do better in future meetings? What can we learn about group work from this meeting?

There are of course many questions one can ask in reviewing meetings and many ways of doing it. One can rotate responsibility for reviewing meetings as long as the reviewer asks questions rather than making pronouncements or judgments. A good way of starting is always to check in: How was it? What went well? What can we improve? I sometimes ask group members to describe their experience in a weather picture or a landscape and then ask them to explain the sunshine, the thunderstorms or the mountain pass that was successfully navigated.

The Action Learning Cycle

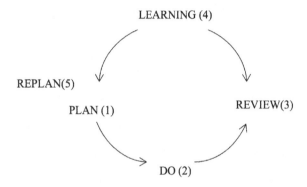

Development in groups or teams happens best through mutual learning. It is important to follow a simple learning cycle of planning, doing, reviewing, learning, and then re-planning. In this way a group or committee will gradually increase its skill and sensitivity, becoming evermore adept in the art of conversation. The team will also acquire confidence in itself and a higher level of trust because common learning reduces the need for gossip and allows difficult situations to be discussed with ever less fear.

Group Leadership

Frequently groups think of leadership as consisting of the chairperson, ignoring the multitude of leadership functions which a successful team, committee or group needs to exercise. If leadership is seen as residing in one person, all too often the outcome is determined by the skills of that person. In mature and effective groups, all team members feel responsible and exercise some leadership.

Single Leadership

 Shared Leadership And Responsibility

In Waldorf school meetings—faculty, Board and major committees —I suggest three formal roles. There is the *chairperson*, who prepares the agenda, begins and chairs the meeting and helps the group to achieve its goals. This role is one of guiding and facilitating the meeting, not controlling or coercing the conversation. The best chairpeople are those who have a clear head for procedure and a good process sense, moving the meeting along and yet making sure everyone has the space and the encouragement to speak. Generally speaking, it is not a good idea to rotate the chairing function between meetings for standing committees or groups because someone needs to feel responsible for the agenda, and chairing is a learned skill which not everyone has. Allow a person to chair for one to two years before exploring who else in now suited to take on this important task. Discuss the role together and the qualities needed to fulfill it and then ask someone to accept this responsibility. Do not rely on volunteers because then the group is unable to explore together who is the right person for this task at this time.

A second formal function is that of the *process advisor or coach*, a role which can be rotated between meetings. Because the chairperson is busy chairing the meeting, it is important to have someone feel responsible for the process—sensing when things are stuck or why someone feels hurt. They can either be part of the meeting or observe but in any case if they are too engaged in the discussion or the decision, they lose their insight and objectivity. The process coach observes the quality of relationships, the speaking and listening and the procedure and evolution of the meeting. He needs to have the right and responsibility of asking questions or intervening to support the development of the group during the meeting. Typical observations include:

- How is it going with time? There are still two significant items on the agenda.
- Mary has been trying to speak for some time. Can we give her a chance?

- There is something going on between Helen and Larry that is affecting the mood. Can the two of you share with us?

Often the process coach can also guide the review process at the end because he or she has been observing and listening carefully.

The third formal role is that of the *scribe or note taker* who will note the decisions made and who has taken on what responsibilities for action. For Board, College and Faculty meetings, it is important to have typed minutes which can be reviewed briefly at the beginning of the next meeting.

Individuals bring a variety of qualities into a meeting. If we liken a conversation to a concert, then we each play an instrument—some a clarinet or flute, others the violin, drum or trumpet. The instruments in an orchestra are grouped in sections, the string section: the violins, violas, and cello; the wind instruments: flute, clarinet, oboe; the brass section: horns, trumpet and trombone. In larger meetings of the full faculty and staff, I think something similar happens. While we each have our own instrument—our unique combination of personality, soul orientation and temperament—we play together with other instruments in sections. A number of people are quite talkative with a strong sense of procedure. Another group is quieter but strongly oriented toward listening and supporting, while a third initiates, speaks a lot and drives the meeting forward.

We have previously noted that a group works at three main levels:

1) the content level of ideas, concepts, examples, stories and argument (thinking)
2) the relational level of feelings, values and attitudes (feeling)
3) the procedural level of aims, goals and intentions (willing).

If we examine each of these dimensions more clearly, we can see that each contains a polarity. With content, the polarity is between ideas and concepts (abstract) and stories and examples (concrete). With relationships this polarity is expressed between speaking/initiating and listening/supporting/nurturing. With procedure it is aims/goals and review/summarizing—where are we going and where are we now?

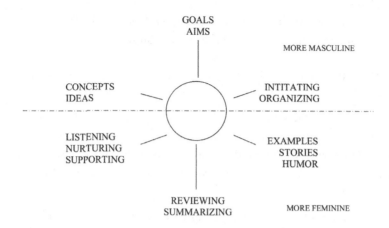

GOALS
AIMS

MORE MASCULINE

CONCEPTS
IDEAS

INTITATING
ORGANIZING

LISTENING
NURTURING
SUPPORTING

EXAMPLES
STORIES
HUMOR

REVIEWING
SUMMARIZING

MORE FEMININE

Qualities of Group Leadership/Soul Orientations

A healthy, balanced conversation needs all of the qualities expressed in these polarities. If there is too much speaking and initiating and not enough listening, chaos results. If there is too much listening, nothing happens. If there are too many examples and not enough combining ideas, we get lost in the woods. If the group is too goal-oriented or reviews too much, life is squeezed out. The effect is like asking a bicycle rider how he is able to pedal, steer and stay balanced all at the same time.

Most groups will have all of these qualities distributed among their members. In my experience, we have all of them in our soul but have one dominant and two secondary qualities. It is interesting and important to bring to consciousness which of these qualities we naturally possess and therefore can offer to the world. Some people have a strong organizing (Mars) orientation, combined with goal awareness (Saturn) and a lot of humor and stories (Mercury). Others have a listening/healing orientation (Venus) as dominant, combined with conceptual clarity and a love of ideas (Jupiter) or an ability to hold on to things, to summarize or ask where a group is (Moon). If groups recognize that each of these qualities is important to healthy functioning, then they begin to recognize that each person has an important leadership role to play. To strive for balance, the harmonizing Sun influence then becomes a joint responsibility.[6]

These leadership and planetary qualities are soul orientations which we possess as individuals and can offer to the group. We also, of course, have our temperaments and our unique personalities, so how we bring these qualities into the conversation will vary. The qualities of ideas, goals, and initiating—Jupiter (God of Wisdom), Saturn (Father Time) and Mars (God of War)—have a more masculine aspect while listening and nurturing (Venus, Goddess of Love), summarizing, reflecting (Moon) and humor, stories and examples (Mercury, Messenger of the Gods and God of Thieves),have a more feminine side. A way of reviewing meetings is to explore the balance between these masculine and feminine qualities.

In working with different groups, I have had the chance to observe both all-male and all-female groups. It always strikes me that groups of women, when doing a task, spend a good bit of time creating life and establishing relationships before moving to the task whereas for men doing the task defines life and relationships. Both are equally effective in accomplishing a goal, but the road taken is very different.

Chapter IV Exercises:

Soul Qualities in Groups: What are my dominant qualities? (40 minutes total)

Take a sheet of paper. Reflect on what qualities you typically bring into a group conversation and note them. See if you can distinguish one dominant and two or three subordinate qualities. (10 minutes)

Then share your thoughts with a friend or colleague and listen to their self-assessment. You are free to comment on each other's views. (10 minutes)

Each person shares what they have come to in the whole group; allow some discussion. (20–30 minutes)

Group Review: Qualities of Leadership (35–40 minutes)

At the end of a meeting use the qualities of group leadership to review the group process. Give individuals 5 minutes to note the balance between masculine and feminine qualities and to describe which qualities were strongly present in the meeting, connected to which group members, and which qualities need strengthening in the future. Share and discuss in the whole group. (30 minutes)

Playing the Symphony: Group Decision Making

Let me return to the orchestral metaphor. We are each an instrument (a certain combination of soul qualities) and we tend to play our instruments together with other violins, woodwinds, or brass instruments (sections or sub-groups). We have a chairperson (the conductor) and a first violinist (the process coach). In conversation we play notes (the content: words, ideas), and we create melodies (the harmony or disharmony of our likes and dislikes) according to a certain rhythm (the procedure).

The planning of the meeting is important because it determines the particular score we are playing together. Without a common score or piece of music, we create chaos.

The chairperson (conductor) helps us to enter at the right time (regulating speaking and listening) and keeps us to a proper tempo (procedure). Just as a piece of music, a symphony let us say, has particular parts to it, so too does the meeting of a Board, faculty or a committee. The clearer we are about the phases of this conversation, the more successful the concert. The *19th Century Symphony*, for example, has four main parts: the overture, which sounds the theme; a first movement in which the theme is elaborated in different ways; a second, usually quicker movement in which variations and sub-themes are developed; and then a final movement. Similarly a group conversation has four main parts: the planning phase in which the topics and aims of the meeting are explored and clarified; an informational part in which we illuminate the question under consideration from various points of view, bringing together all relevant facts; a judging, weighing phase in which we explore relevant criteria and values; and then a concluding phase in which we state conclusions or make decisions. At the outset it is important to know whether we are seeking to arrive at a conclusion— why the teacher evaluation policy was not followed in this case—or making a decision—we will modify the policy by adding a new step to the process. Conclusions are past-oriented while decisions are future-oriented, asking us to translate the decision taken into deed. Many groups who are not sufficiently aware of procedure will jump from describing a problem to a discussion of options for solving it before they have properly explored causes. Or more commonly, some members of the group will be looking for causes while others will be exploring remedies, causing confusion in the group.

Problem Analysis: Causes (Past)
Planning (Creating Focus and Warmth)
Topic: The Winter Fair
Aim: To understand why there was a 20% drop in revenue in 2010 from the previous year (Causes)

Picture Building / Brainstorming (Gathering information—Light)
- "It rained on Saturday."
- "There were fewer items made by the parent craft group."
- "The more expensive items were displayed at the back of the hall."
- "Publicity was late."
- "There wasn't a raffle."

Judging / Weighing (Sharing values—Water)

What is the most relevant information and why? "The raffle brought in $1800 last year. Its absence hurt us."

- "I think the poor publicity and the lack of salable items made the difference."
- "There wasn't as much enthusiasm this year because fewer parents were involved in making things."
- (Publicity and enthusiasm were considered key criteria.)

Conclusion: Late publicity and less involvement of parents were the key causes of decreased revenue.

Review of Meeting
- Decision making—Future

Planning:
Topic: Winter Fair
Aim: Steps to increase success

Information Sharing: Alternative Decisions
- Require all parents to make things.
- Increase the size of fair committee.
- Begin the parent craft groups work in early September.
- Have publicity out by the middle of October and have a follow-up a month later.
- Create a separate raffle committee.

Judging Effectiveness of Alternatives:
- A discussion of the relative merits of different proposals
- Judgment criteria: changes with maximum impact, least drain on community.

Decision
- Start craft groups earlier and have at least one per grade.
- Create raffle subcommittee.
- Begin publicity in late September.

If we reflect on the four stages or movements of group decision-making, we can notice that they really describe the qualities of any creation process. First we need interest and enthusiasm for writing the paper, doing the painting or starting a school. The quality of commitment, of enthusiasm, of fire is needed. Then we gather information and resources. We begin experimenting with different colors, gathering central thoughts or quotes and writing or, in the case of a school, acquiring insight into the marvelous qualities of the Waldorf curriculum (light). Then we enter a phase of judging or weighing, a watery uncertain time—the painting needs more form and more red, the ending of the essay is weak, should the school be downtown or in the suburbs, and when will we have enough money to begin? Finally we come to a conclusion or decision—the red fits there and now I'm finished, or I will end the essay with the quote and retype it, or St. James Episcopal Church has a perfect space for us, enough for a kindergarten and four grades and we can begin next September. The creation process has gone through the fire of will through light, to water and finally come to earth, manifesting in deeds.

> Planning—Fire—Enthusiasm
>
> Information Gathering—Light/Air
>
> Judging/Weighing—Water
>
> Concluding/Deciding—Earth[7]

Part of the reason that reports from committees in a larger meeting are dead is because we convey only the conclusion or decision, the earth element, without all the life that went into it. So it is best to keep reports to a minimum and to add a comment or two about the process in getting to the conclusion or decision.

Decision Making by Consensus

In any group process it is the differences of opinion about what went wrong or what we should do now that generate tension and disagreement. It is in this judging phase that our differences in viewpoint and values become manifest. When we make decisions by voting, there is no opportunity to explore these differences and the majority carries the day. In that sense voting is a way of legitimizing conflict. While the expectation exists that the minority will play along and not be bad sports, in collegial institutions like Waldorf schools there is no clear hierarchy that can function as an enforcer, and controversial decisions have a way of not being whole-heartedly carried by the full faculty and staff. It therefore makes sense, practically as well as philosophically, to work with a consensus process of decision-making, a process in which everyone has an opportunity to speak to the issue and to clarify their reasons for a particular viewpoint. After both working with and observing consensus decision making for many years, I think it is important to be aware of the following principles:

1) Use a formal consensus decision-making process for all important decisions. For minor issues, just check in—is it okay to proceed in this way?

2) As you enter a consensus process, remind people that everyone will have a chance to speak and that having spoken, each person will decide whether he or she supports the decision, whether they have

reservations but would not block or whether they will block because they cannot in good conscience go along with what is being proposed.

3) In a consensus process it is important to recognize three distinct steps in the consensus process itself. This does not negate the need to consider the four phases of procedure referred to previously.

- The initial discussion of the question.

- The formulation of a proposed action or decision by the chairperson or someone else skilled at capturing the "sense of the meeting."

- A speaking to the proposal by everyone in the room, stating whether they approve, question or oppose and their reasons for doing so.

4) Before checking where people stand, it is good to remind everyone that people are here to act in the best interests of the school and the children. It is also appropriate at such times to have a moment of silence and to ask for spiritual guidance from the spiritual beings who accompany and bless this school.

5) Do not rush the meeting for a decision. Allow up to three meetings for important decisions.

6) Have a policy in place which allows you as a Board or a faculty to move forward with a decision in the absence of consensus after two or three meetings. It could be that you say we will proceed with consensus minus 2 or 3 or that you will resort to a ¾ majority vote on such occasions.

7) Be careful not to demonize the dissenting voice. I have on a number of occasions witnessed an opposition of one person to consensus which by the next week was seen to be fully justified. Equally, recognize that you cannot block too often. If the same person is repeatedly blocking consensus, the chairperson, convener or process observer may need to convene a special meeting to explore with the individual what it is that is happening to him or her in the group.

A consensus decision-making process entered into honestly and with understanding will build community and commitment. It is a way of honoring both the members of the school community and the spirit of truth as it manifests in each of us.[8]

Group Development

All social creations—relationships, groups, institutions and societies—share a developmental cycle of birth, growth and transformation. In the case of working groups, I experience three main levels of development. The first is a meeting and adjustment phase. We arrive as a new member on a board or a committee, perhaps with a few other new members, and we look around. The image I have of such a situation is like a medieval tournament, the knights wearing their armor for protection and the ladies multicolored scarves for allure—except that we are all knights and ladies being both protected and on our best behavior. In such situations we ask ourselves who is here, do I fit in, will I be liked, who do I get along with, am I needed, do I have something to offer and a host of other questions. Over the course of a few meetings we develop a sense of our own place, who we naturally align with and who we regard as sensible, who is awkward or difficult and what issues tend to be contentious. Informal sub-groups tend to form and we acquire a set of habits as a group—we all come five minutes late, chat quickly and draw up our chairs on similar sides of the table. Tom chairs the meeting, Sally is the first to react on any issue, Helen waits until we are almost done to raise a point of objection and so on—all of this is semiconscious.

In this first phase of development we are individually aware of relational issues, of likes and dislikes, of personality conflicts in the group, but we are content and procedure-oriented, avoiding the emotional issues in the interests of getting on with things. We have become an *adjusted working group* in which the interesting learning and review, as well as the emotional venting happens with our friends in the car on the way home or later on the telephone but not in the group itself.

Most working groups never move beyond the task orientation of the adjusted working group, bearing the existing limitations stoically, not realizing there are other possibilities. The emotional relational dimension, while visible in hugs, jokes, disagreements, scowls or angry outbursts, is avoided because the group doesn't know how to deal with it. If the group reviews its process regularly or has a skilled chairperson or a good outside facilitator, it will be able to cross the threshold into the domain of feelings and perceptions. When this step becomes conscious, the group enters a second major phase in its development in which relational process issues are dealt with in the group rather than outside of it. If the first phase could be described as the adjusted working group, I would call this phase the *experience group*.

Perception-Sharing Exercise

As a help to opening the relational dimension in a conscious way, I often recommend having every group member consciously prepare and share their perceptions of other group members, using the following kinds of questions:

1) What do I admire about how you work in the group (1 or 2 qualities)?

2) What would I have you do less of or transform?

3) What new quality or gift would I give you?

Have the whole group write down the answers to these questions for each other before sharing, preferably a day or two before. Then go one by one, all eight or nine group members address one person, then the next person, until everyone has received the perceptions of the others. There is no discussion. I have never known this to be anything but a positive experience when consciously prepared because we judge ourselves more severely than others do. It is almost always uplifting and brings warmth and caring.

The quality of the experience group is that it is able to handle task and relationships at the same time. If two people are at each other, the group can stop the process, facilitate an exploration of the issues and then move on. It develops the skills and confidence to touch on the feeling dimensions of group life. In such a group, reviews are honest, feedback is direct and there is limited gossiping outside the group. Experience groups typically create a strong sense of commitment among members because their relational issues as well as task issues are worked with consciously.[9]

The ability to move into this phase of development in groups involves meeting more deeply and crossing a threshold of fear. We fear both the perceptions and opinions of others and the need to be responsible for and public about our own likes and dislikes. Yet the practice of caring involves becoming aware of our likes and dislikes and dealing with them responsibly when they affect our working together with others in negative ways. When we are in meetings full of semiconscious animosities and hurts, do we really think that positive working spiritual beings can work? The space becomes psychologically and spiritually polluted, asking us to acquire the ability to do spring cleaning so that the sun can shine through the windows. Doing spring cleaning means that all of the group members have the freedom and the responsibility to stop a process that is emotionally damaging by asking for a pause and asking the individuals involved to speak clearly about what is going on for them, using "I statements" and not blaming others. This can clear the air in five minutes if limited to the issue at hand, and then the meeting can move on. It is also in the realm of relationships and feelings that the practice of a good review can be enormously helpful and that the process advisor or coach is essential as an impartial observer and helper.

Through the ability to work with relationships more consciously, the group develops warmth and commitment to each other. We stop criticizing each other in the hallway or on the way home, and we develop more interest in each other. Often sharing parts of our biography can support a deepening interest. Spending five to ten minutes each meeting allowing one or two people to address a biography question can increase mutual understanding.

Some Biography-Sharing Questions

1) How did I come to Waldorf education?
2) What started me on my inner journey?
3) Share a picture of yourself at age 6: your favorite room, clothes, person.
4) Who were your heroes and heroines in adolescence?
5) Describe three people who have played significant roles in your life.
6) What were the spoken or unspoken commandments in your home when you were an adolescent, and how do they live in you now?
7) What gives you joy in your work now?

It is good if everyone can work with the same question and after you are done find a new question to share. The opportunities for such structured sharing can be created easily and will add life and enjoyment to the meeting. The faculty, Finance committee, Board or Parent Council, once it has acquired the ability to have effective meetings in which both tasks and relationships can be worked with well, will notice growing interest in how the needs of both the individual and the school community can be met. This mutually supportive relationship between the individual and the community was clearly expressed by Rudolf Steiner in The Motto of The Social Ethic:

> The healing social life is only found when in the mirror of each human soul the whole community finds its reflection and when in the community the virtue of each one is living.

When people are met and seen in the group and community, the individual feels called upon to serve the community with her or his talents, as the community is then experienced as the soil in which we can each realize our deepest intentions. Entering into the level of the will—what can we do together to serve the whole and what can we do to serve each other's development—becomes the third basic level of development in the group. I would call this the *creative maturity* of the group. In working with a few groups who have achieved this level of caring, energy and creativity, I have noticed high commitment, joy and an amazing ability to get work done. Such groups can function as a blessing for the whole community and for their members. They help each other find new direction in life, and they dream and do tasks beyond the task descriptions of their particular mandate.

Thinking Level—Adjusted Working Group

Feeling Level—Experience Group

Will Level—Mature Creative Group

I need to also mention that when groups disband or when there is a large shift in committee, faculty or Board membership, then it is helpful to plan a conscious ending, to review the work accomplished and to give thanks to each other for the experience of being together.

A different but similar framework for looking at stages of group development was proposed by Bruce Tuckman in 1965. He describes four stages, forming (beginning and adjusted group), norming (adjusted working group), storming (experience group) and performing (mature group). These terms are easy to remember and can help us to identify where we are in process.[10]

There are a number of activities which can help groups to move forward and to enjoy each other. One of these is working with the arts. Eurythmy and singing are particularly helpful as they bring to consciousness a strong community element—in moving together and in combining our individual voices to create a harmonious whole; in a round, a simple melody or a four part choral piece. Rudolf Steiner suggests that the sculptural arts teach us formative principles in building institutions, that painting and eurythmy bring us into the realm of relationships, whereas the musical arts help us to experience the essential nature of community life.[11]

Games serve a complementary function to the arts in developing humor and playfulness. They allow us to experience each other in less serious ways, to be children and to practice trust and cooperation. Adapting children's games for a five-minute refresher—such as elbow tag or musical chairs—creates both breathlessness and new energy after sitting too long.

The importance of sharing biography work and exercises has already been described. In addition, developing group norms or practices can bring more consciousness to the process of working together. I once worked with Wainwright House, an adult education and conference center in Rye, New York. They adopted a list of receptive listening practices which included: Listen with Trust, Listen with Empathy and Listen with Patience. Speak from I, Share the Floor and Maintain Confidentiality. Each group can develop its own norms and practices which can then be used periodically in the review of meetings.

Authentic Conversation and Spiritual Communion

I have explored the psychological, technical and more external aspects of dialog and group work. Now I would like to touch on the interior or spiritual dimension of working together in community. A starting point is to recognize that there is no social situation devoid of psychological and spiritual realities. If we can accept this, then the challenge for all of us in Waldorf school communities becomes one of how to work together in such a way that a temple is created in which positive working spirits can be present. These beings are deeply interested in our activities and long to be able to converse with us in new ways. Positive working spirits can do so only if we are active co-creators with them, for they need to safeguard our freedom. Rudolf Steiner describes this new possibility of co-creation in the following way:

> Thus human associations are the secret places where higher spiritual beings descend in order to work through individuals, just as the soul works through the body.[12]

I believe there are two main paths for groups seeking to enter into a conscious dialog, a conscious communion, with the spiritual world. The first is sacramental communion, practiced in a variety of religious and church settings in which a priest or religious person invokes the spiritual world through a prescribed set of ritualistic acts. The other is spiritual communion, in which the group works together in such a way that their words and deeds lift human experience to a higher spiritual level. In describing the differences in these two paths, Rudolf Steiner stated:

> I would put it thus—the community of the cultus (sacramental communion) seeks to draw the angels of heaven down to the place where the ritual is being celebrated so that they may be present in the congregation, whereas the anthroposophical community [or Waldorf community] seeks to lift human souls into the supersensible realms so that they may enter into the company of angels.[13]

The sacramental ritual of the Christian churches proceeds from the reading of the gospel (revelation of the divine world) to the offering (of physical bread and wine), to the transubstantiation (of the bread and the wine into Christ's body), and finally, to communion (into the community of Christian souls through the taking of the bread and wine). This is a powerful and ever-renewing act for a community of believers.

Spiritual communion or authentic conversation can also be seen as occurring in stages. The first stage is one of initially coming together, let us say on a Tuesday evening at 8:00pm in the sixth grade classroom. We may enter full of the business of the day, tired and slightly out of sorts, but we also can stop for a moment and recognize that we are entering a potentially sacred space and take a moment to collect ourselves. Then we can quietly behold each other and be aware that we are divine as well as earthly beings. To recognize, to remember that each of us is a revelation of the divine, now clad in the cloak of this particular body and with this personality, can give us both patience and reverence. It is not easy to create this mood in ourselves, especially toward those whom we regard with dislike. But with practice and interest we can experience this mood and this possibility with every person we encounter.

In the next phase we begin a conversation, a dialog. Here we are called upon to understand the other, to listen to the melodies of different thoughts and feelings. To develop understanding we need to make an offering, to turn our attention to the other, to experience for a moment "I am thou." As I experience this stage of group conversation in myself, I have to open a space in myself, still my thoughts and reactions to let the other live in me. It is tiring because I need to be both still and focused on the other, not allowing my attention to wander. When I speak then, I need to know what is essential to be expressed, what is my truth and that of the group at this moment. It is another kind of offering—not saying that which pops into my mind but expressing that which is essential for the group to move forward. In listening, we sacrifice living with our own thoughts and feelings, and in speaking the essential, we give up the fullness and diversity of our inner soul dialog.

In *The Inner Aspect of the Social Question,* Rudolf Steiner describes an activity which captures the mood of the offering, of listening, of attending to the other out of the Christian tradition:

> In whatever the least of your brethren thinks, you must recognize that I am thinking in Him, and that I enter into your feeling whenever you bring another's thought into relation with

your own, and whenever you feel a fraternal interest for what is passing in another's soul. Whatever opinion, whatever outlook on life, you discover in the least of your brethren, therein you are seeking thyself.[14]

In listening and speaking with genuine care, we create a mood of reverence toward each other which allows us to be freer, to act out of our higher selves, to say and hear things full of wisdom. Working in this way can overcome many obstacles between us and invites the participation and the blessing of angels.

The third stage of spiritual communion in community is achieved when, out of our mutual understanding and empathy, we are able to act toward each other and toward the whole group out of compassion and love. In his poetic book *Human Encounters and Karma*, Athys Floride writes:

> This stage, which corresponds to the Transubstantiation, must be willed; to do so will take all the strength we possess. The perception of the other, of our bond with the other, now becomes deeper. We enter the realm where the forces of Karma are at work. Now we can strive to understand the impulses, the currents bringing us together with other human beings.[15]

This transubstantiation occurs when the members of the group—the faculty, Board or Parent Committee—each acknowledge in themselves that I am here with my destiny partners, and I am asked to give to the group and to each member what is needed for our mutual development. It rests on the deeply felt knowledge expressed by Martin Luther King and cited at the beginning of this chapter.

> All men are caught in an inescapable network of mutuality, tied in a single garment of destiny. Whatever affects one directly affects all indirectly. I can never be what I ought to be until you are what you ought to be. And you can never be what you ought to be until I am what I ought to be.

In having been part of the Sunbridge College Core Group for many years—the main spiritual and decision-making body of the College—I often had a sense of joy and recognition that I was part of a destiny community which asked me to give more of myself and out of a higher part of myself than would normally have been the case. At times this allowed us to act toward each other in ways which were deeply loving and yet not sentimental.

The fourth stage of a spiritual communion process is the experience of communion, the felt presence of the spirit. We have all had momentary experiences of spiritual communion in conversations and in groups, a feeling of magical presence, of a star-filled space.

When the previously described qualities and moods are present— the recognition of the divine in each of us, the offering of our attention through conscious listening and speaking and the deeply felt recognition of our karmic bond and mutual indebtedness (transubstantiation)—then we invite the presence and blessing of spiritual beings who offer us communion.[16] Such a development can take place over the course of many conversations or it can occur in one meeting, through grace.

While experiences of spiritual communion in conversation occur for individuals and groups through grace, it is also possible to cultivate an understanding, a sense for the attitudes, moods and actions which make spiritual communion possible in all Waldorf school communities and in other institutions seeking to serve the needs of this time. It is, I believe, a question of awareness and practice. An increasing number of groups are working consciously on the task of building spiritual community, including M. Scott Peck and the Foundation for Community Encouragement, Parker Palmer and Otto Scharmer, Peter Senge and Joseph Jaworski at the Society for Organizational Learning at the Massachusetts Institute of Techology (MIT). In addition there are the many dialog groups based on the work of David Bohm.[17] Scharmer in particular, in *Theory U: Leading from the Future as It Emerges*, describes seven steps in the U process, from downloading to seeing, sensing, presencing, crystallizing, prototyping and performing.[18] The four field structures of attention or consciousness which he describes, and which are most relevant to "spiritual communion," refer to how we listen or attend in social situations, in particular groups. Scharmer states that "every action by a person, a leader, a group, an organization or a community can be enacted in these four ways."[19] The first field Scharmer describes as "I in me," or downloading where we hear and articulate our habitual pictures or judgments. The second is captured by the phrase "I in it," which signifies a willingness to see and understand others, to attend to the factual world. This type of awareness in a group leads to conversations characterized by discussion and debate. The third type of awareness is characterized by an open mind, by suspending judgments and truly meeting the other which Scharmer describes as "I in you," as empathic listening. This can create genuine dialog in which "we begin to see how the world unfolds through someone else's eyes. …We move from discussing the objective world of things, figures and facts into the story of a living being, a living system, and self." The fourth field is "I in now," speaking from the future and connecting to "the beings that surround us."[20] This activity, this conversation has the quality of presencing. If we look at the images and process of individual and group development which Scharmer describes, we can recognize again the four steps of spiritual communion, but couched in more evidence- based language and concepts.

Another very helpful and complementary perspective on spiritual conversation was developed at a series of conferences in the late 1990s on group synergy and collective intelligence sponsored by the Fetzer Institute and the Institute of Noetic Sciences. A summary report by Robert Kenny describes a clear horizontal and vertical dimension to spiritual communion, reflecting both a concern about the quality of human relationships and mutual authenticity between people (horizontal) and a joint commitment to working with spirit (vertical).[21] The conditions which he mentions include:

- A mutual commitment to each other and a clear and shared human and spiritual purpose
- Developing an atmosphere of safety, confidentiality, trust and respect
- Speaking from the heart and out of experience
- Inclusivity and respect toward different human and spiritual orientations

- A willingness to play
- An ability to deal with differences and with conflict
- Creating a sacred space open to guidance and inspiration
- A joint commitment to inner development and learning
- A meeting that is prepared, held and guided by a clear process and form of facilitation

When these conditions are met, a true chalice has been created through which group members can experience:

- An enhanced level of trust in self and others
- A sense of being known and seen
- A greater sense of authenticity and creativity
- A sense of spiritual presence and guidance
- Mutual encouragement
- Satisfaction at connecting inner values with life
- An increased desire to serve and contribute to a better world
- A greater sense of individual and community health[21]

These are also the conditions and effects of spiritual communion so clearly and simply described by Rudolf Steiner in the America or Threefold Verse given to Ralph Courtney, an early student of anthroposophy and one of the founders of the Threefold Community in Spring Valley, New York:

> May our feeling penetrate into the center of our heart and seek in love to unite itself with human beings sharing the same goals, and with spirit beings, who bearing grace and strengthening us from realms of light and illuminating our love, are gazing down upon our earnest, heartfelt striving.

The Practice of Community

True community is characterized by integrity, and integrity is not without pain. As M. Scott Peck notes in *The Different Drum*, community "requires that we let matters rub up against each other, that we fully experience the tension of conflicting needs, demands and interests, that we can be emotionally torn apart by them."[22] Without the experience of this pain and struggle we do not develop. Individual development occurs most honestly in community, for it is here that we encounter our dark sides and practice knowing and caring for each other.

In this exploration of working together, we began by describing the mystery of conversation, of dialog, and then looked at the psychological and practical aspects of group work before turning to the question of sacramental conversation. Each level supports the next one: We need to be willing to engage in community, to suffer the pain of misunderstanding in order to enter the realm of conversation; conversation is the medium of group work; and working with consciousness and sensitivity in groups enhances the possibility of spiritual communion.

I often experience in Waldorf school communities a longing for spiritual community and a sense that when we meet we are trying to create a chalice for the spirit. Yet I also frequently experience a lack of form and consciousness in meetings, through a late start, unresolved personal difficulties and a lack of listening so that the blessings of positive working spirits cannot be experienced. Conscious listening and speaking, clarity of meeting focus, skilled facilitation and active participation are what we need to practice continuously in order to create a chalice worthy of grace, of spiritual presence.

Endnotes

1. See Heinz Zimmerman, *Speaking, Listening, Understanding: The Art of Creating Conscious Conversation* (Lindisfarne Press, Hudson, NY, 1996). Also the wonderful book by Paul Matthews, *Sing Me the Creation, A Sourcebook for Poets, Teachers and for All Who Work to Develop the Life of the Imagination* (Hawthorn Press, Stroud, UK, 1994). This book is full of helpful exercises to use, play with and gain wisdom from. Marjorie Spock has also written two important essays: "Reflections on Community Building" and "Goethean Conversation," both available from Rudolf Steiner College Press, Fair Oaks, CA.

2. M.C. Richards, *Centering: In Pottery, Poetry and Person* (Wesleyan University Press, Middletown, CT, 1964), p. 49.

3. See Rudolf Steiner, *Social and Anti-Social Forces in the Human Being* (Mercury Press, Spring Valley, NY, 1987).

4. See David Bohm, *On Dialogue* (Taylor & Francis, London, 1996).

5. Ibid., p. 65.

6. See Bernard Lievegoed, *Man on the Threshold: The Challenge of Inner Development* (Hawthorn Press, Stroud, UK, 1982), pp. 97–118, for a discussion of the planetary processes in the human being. The planetary typology described was first developed by co-workers at the Netherlands Pedagogical Institute (NPI) in Holland in the 1960s.

7. These stages can be compared to Old Saturn, Sun, Moon and Earth as described by Rudolf Steiner in *Occult Science, An Outline* (Anthroposophic Press, Hudson, NY, 1984).

8. Caroline Estes, "Consensus Ingredients," in *Context: A Quarterly of Humane Sustainable Culture*, Fall 1983.

9. See Coover, Deacon, Esser, Moor, *Resource Manual for a Living Revolution* (New Society Press, 1978), pp. 44–79. Also, John Adair, *Action Centered Leadership* (Gower, UK, 1973).

10. Bruce Tuckman, "Developmental Sequences in Small Groups" in *Small Groups: Studies in Social Interaction*, A.P. Hare, E.F. Borgatta and R.F. Bales, eds., (Knopf, New York, 1965).

11. Leo de la Houssaye, *Sozial Kunst und Ihre Quellen* (Verlag Freies Geistesleben, Stuttgart, 1983), pp. 44–76.

12. Rudolf Steiner, *Brotherhood and the Struggle for Existence* (Mercury Press, Spring Valley, NY, 1980), p. 9.

13. Rudolf Steiner, *Awakening to Community* (Anthroposophic Press, Hudson, NY, 1985), p. 157.

14. Rudolf Steiner, *The Inner Aspect of the Social Question* (Anthroposophic Press, Hudson, NY), p. 36.

15. Athys Floride, *Human Encounters and Karma* (Anthroposophic Press, Hudson, NY), p. 31.

16. Rudolf Steiner, The Hague, November 14, 1922.

17. See in particular the stimulating book by M. Scott Peck, *The Different Drum: Community Making and Peace* (Simon and Schuster, NY, 1981), pp. 86–106. Also Friedmann Schwarzkopf, in *Beholding the Nature of Reality: Possibility of Spiritual Community* (Rudolf Steiner College Press, Fair Oaks, CA, 1996), explores the nature of community from a very important cognitive perspective.

18. Otto Scharmer, *Theory U: Leading from Future as It Emerges* (Society for Organizational Learning, Cambridge, MA, 2007).

19. Ibid., p. 11.

20. Ibid., pp. 10–14 and 271–301.

21. Fetzer Institute (Robert Kenny, Group Service and Group Synergy, Kalamazoo, MI, 2000). Also Fetzer Institute, *Centered on the Edge: Mapping a Field of Collective Intelligence and Spiritual Wisdom* (Kalamazoo, MI, 2001).

22. Op. cit., Peck, pp. 77–78.

V

Developing a Culture of Leadership, Learning and Service

Let the commitment and the cause be the place where we work.
— Peter Block

I can summarize my experience working within and outside the Waldorf movement in a provocative way by saying that within the Waldorf movement we have new social imaginations and new social forms, but we often don't work with them out of a new consciousness. Meanwhile, the conventional world has old, hierarchical forms and old imaginations, but, in part because of economic pressure, works at changing them with a new consciousness. It is a compelling experience to work with United Airlines pilots practicing communication skills, paraphrasing and consensus, and to see a dedication I seldom experience in our own institutions. For them, the experience of meeting in new ways is so deeply moving because they can experience each other as human beings for the first time, rather than as roles within a bureaucratic structure. For us such a meeting is assumed, and because it is often not worked at consciously, it falls into habit and drudgery.

I am quite concerned about the state of many Waldorf school communities. Despite many accomplishments, mature Waldorf schools and other institutions connected to anthroposophy often exhibit a tiredness, lack of energy and direction, an absence of leadership and lack of joy that is worrisome. As individuals and institutions inspired by the work of Rudolf Steiner, we have a rich legacy of new social and community forms that are collegial, non-hierarchical, and spiritually based. These forms encourage us to create institutions in which positive working spiritual beings can participate, and they are forms which encourage us to meet at deeper levels, to experience that we are brothers and sisters on a path of mutual development.[1] Yet this rich tradition of new social and community forms alone does not appear sufficient to sustain us or to lend to our work the health and vitality we would wish for at this time. And so we need to ask why, despite this rich social legacy, is there often a sense of tiredness, of drifting?

In reflecting on this question, I see a number of interconnected issues. The first has to do with the question of leadership. As a culture, Waldorf schools often do not seem to understand, value or support leadership. Secondly, despite the growing complexity and maturity of our institutional forms, and the multitude of meetings and committees in which we participate, we tend to have a limited commitment to learning the social and administrative skills necessary to make our non-hierarchical institutions work effectively. Reluctant leadership, poor decision-making forms and limited social skills haunt our efforts to create community. Connected to the resistance to learn the social skills necessary to help our institutions work well is the reluctance to meet humanly at deeper levels, to work on our relationships truthfully so that disagreements can become the basis of healing and transformation. Lastly, while we think of Waldorf schools and other institutions connected to the work of Rudolf Steiner as being committed to service, I am not convinced that we have developed a deeper understanding and commitment to being a service culture, with the important exception of our commitment to children and to child development in the classroom.

In pointing to these limitations, I do not intend to minimize the real accomplishments of many individuals and schools, but rather to call for a re-dedication of effort, a shift in awareness and a greater focus on building effective school communities.

A Cultural and Generational Reflection

In order to better understand these observations, I believe it is important to review the cultural norms of Waldorf education and of anthroposophy as they have evolved in the last decades and to reflect on the attitudes which two different generations active in Waldorf schools bring to questions of leadership.

The nature and experience of leadership in our communities is affected by the fact that many of our institutions have entered an "administrative stage" in their development. Management, administration and leadership have become important because we no longer share the youthful, pioneer days when the spiritual world was working overtime to help us and when we had the charismatic founding personalities of Henry Barnes and Carlo Pietzner or Werner Glas and others to inspire and lead. The question in more mature, established organizations is not how do we survive and acquire the people, land and buildings to do our work. It is more how do we manage what we have. How do we improve administration and how do we develop a new style and a new generation of leadership?

The shift of many of our schools, institutions and communities to a more mature phase of development comes at the same time that a new generation in their thirties and forties is entering into and having positions of responsibility, while an older "Boomer" generation reluctantly gives way. These older colleagues see themselves as the builders of the Waldorf School Movement and have strong anti-authoritarian and anti-leadership biases reinforced by experiences with their often-charismatic predecessors. While in part reluctant leaders, this older generation developed what I would call the leadership of the work horses who under the veneer of collegial and group leadership carried out the required leadership tasks, often at great personal sacrifice. Mostly women, this generation of Waldorf school leaders did not concern itself very much with either clarifying leadership roles and responsibilities or in consciously selecting or reviewing people in leadership positions. A younger generation, sometimes called Generation X, is less willing to sacrifice their personal lives for the school and along with parents is pushing for a clear definition of roles and responsibilities and reasonable workloads and pay. It is to be hoped that the older generation can make space for and mentor those with new energy and new ideas while sharing their valuable insights and experience.

I also experience a psychological issue that works against developing a learning culture in our communities. Being on a path of inner development increases an individual's awareness of the gap between what we could be and what we are. If we add the pressures of time and responsibility and the millennial urgency of the times, then we can easily be led into dogmatism and to an anti-psychological orientation, both of which defend us against our own insecurities.

Another essential aspect of the culture of Waldorf school communities and of anthroposophical institutions is that anthroposophy is a cultural movement. We're largely a movement of teachers, thinkers and artists, with the exception of the biodynamic and curative movements. If we look at anthroposophy as an incarnating being of head, heart and limbs, or of cultural life, social life and economic life, we are by and large a cultural movement in North America. Many business people who meet us are not comfortable and don't feel welcomed, a feeling shared by those individuals who carry a strong concern about questions of social justice. The consequences of our cultural orientation as a spiritual and educational movement are quite far-reaching. Leaders are heads that talk well. The Anthroposophical Society has the purpose of creating true meetings between human beings, yet the main form that we have chosen to do this is the study group.

As I am primarily a teacher, perhaps I can ask some questions which make our cultural and vocational one-sidedness visible. Are teachers strongly interested in learning from others and sharing? Are teachers interested in administration and economics? Are they interested in group process, or leadership or management? Are they interested in a deeper heart meeting between people? Yes, to some degree, but the vocation is primarily one of individuals working with their students to awaken an interest in a particular subject, to pass on knowledge already acquired. I think many of our strengths and weaknesses as a movement stem from the vocational orientation and one-sidedness of the teacher, thinker and artist.

If these cultural reflections are largely true, then we face significant challenges in developing the insights, attitudes and skills necessary to promote a more conscious culture of leadership, of learning and of service within Waldorf schools and within the broader anthroposophical movement.

Encouraging Leadership

As a first step in developing a new culture of leadership, we can raise to consciousness what our image of leadership is and then search for a conception of leadership that fits the needs of self-administered schools and communities. I think we carry mostly an old image of leadership—the charismatic male leadership of the founders, or the more manipulative command and control leadership of the corporate world. Not wanting this, we retreat into an ideology of collegiality—of everybody needing to be involved in everything—and fall into a morass of meetings, inadequate decision making, chaos and conflict. Leadership is present, but people exercising leadership functions such as Faculty Chair, Board President or Personnel Committee Head feel undermined and often regret exercising initiative.

If we could embrace the notion of leadership as stewardship or understand the concept of servant leadership as developed by Robert Greenleaf, perhaps we could breathe more easily and acknowledge that we both need leadership and actually have leadership capacities within our circle of colleagues. The central notion of both stewardship and servant leadership as Peter Block notes in his excellent book, *Stewardship*, is "to choose service over self-interest."[2] Robert Greenleaf writes that servant leadership "begins with the natural feeling that one wants to serve, to serve first—the best test is do those served grow as persons, do they, while being served become healthier, wiser, freer, more autonomous, more likely themselves to become servants."[3] The most important qualities of the servant leader for both Greenleaf and Block include listening, empathy, awareness, persuasion, conceptualization, foresight and stewardship.[4]

In addition to having a broader and more conscious conception of leadership appropriate to the values of Waldorf education, we need to delegate leadership responsibilities consciously. This is often not done in our institutions. We usually let people volunteer because everyone's tired. Leadership is then given to those who are willing to serve on four committees rather than on one, and if they serve long enough, they will have the experience and the power to be effective leaders. The result can be that leadership is not explicit and that the best people may not be asked. The type of leadership desired is not discussed, and people are often not freed up from other tasks to provide effective leadership.

The inability to define and consciously give leadership responsibilities based on competence is a weakness in many of our schools. It may be due to our not wanting to limit people's freedom, or because of a certain reluctance to enter the realm of administrative clarity. In any case, the tendency towards unclarity leads to undermining leadership and to the hidden exercise of power or to what I think of as the hidden but absolutely real power of the "work horses" previously mentioned.

Questions about Leadership

It can be useful to reflect on the following questions about leadership in our schools and communities:

1. Who exercises what leadership responsibilities in our institution?
2. How are leadership positions defined?
3. How are leaders selected?
4. What type of leadership do we want in different positions?
5. What criteria and what process of selection do we require?
6. Will individuals be given the time and support to carry out their functions?
7. What education or training is provided for leadership?
8. How will the exercise of leadership be reviewed?
9. Can more experienced people mentor those in new leadership roles?
10. Can we make the exercise of leadership a rewarding activity by thanking those who have accepted additional responsibility?

Toward a Culture of Learning

In addition to the question of leadership, many Waldorf schools face the question of how to develop more of a learning culture among the adult members of the community. The further development of the Anthroposophical Society and the School of Spiritual Science with a renewed focus on research is an important beginning because it encourages a modest exploration of where we are with our inner and outer work. If this beginning can be further strengthened, it has the effect of sanctioning a deeper explorative research orientation.

A second dimension of developing a learning culture is to recognize that our collegial, non-hierarchical institutions require a high level of "practical social understanding," to use Rudolf Steiner's phrase, a high level of social skill.[5] This means learning from experience, reviewing committee forms, decision-making procedures, the exercise of leadership and learning in an ongoing way about group process. Why do these forms work? What should the function of a chairperson be? Do we also need a process coach? How do we improve listening and communication skills? How do we work with disagreements and conflicts? To be interested in community building, in the art of social creation, means an ongoing commitment to learning from our social experiences; it means weekly and monthly and yearly reviews to assess what is working well and what isn't.

In addition to learning from our experiences, it is important to avail ourselves of the many fine psychological insights and community-building methods of other groups. What comes to mind is the work of M. Scott Peck and the Foundation for Community Encouragement, the approaches to servant leadership developed by the Robert Greenleaf Center, decision making by consensus stemming from the Quaker tradition and the many insights of humanistic psychology. We can also learn from the field of management and of non-profit administration, in particular about the realm of Board responsibilities.[6]

Developing this kind of learning and sharing means overcoming our aversion to psychology, being interested in what other groups and institutions have done and developing a learning network between Waldorf schools, curative communities, CSAs, adult education centers and cooperatively-run businesses. This is an exciting challenge for the Waldorf movement at a time when it has entered a new stage of institutional maturity.

Part of the challenge of learning in our institutions is to encourage conscious mutual development. Many conventional organizations ask their employees to meet with their superiors and their peers in quarterly and annual performance reviews. While such practices can be punitive, they have the virtue of creating a conscious assessment process. In our institutions we could create annual individual development plans that each individual writes down, based on conversations with colleagues.

In addition to a description of work responsibilities for each teacher, receptionist or development coordinator, it could include three basic aspects:

1. Our aims and goals regarding inner development, for example: working with Steiner's six exercises, observing nature twice a week, developing a deeper knowledge of the stars, having fifteen minutes of quiet every morning.

2. Our aims as social beings, for example: improving our facilitation skills, working on listening, working through our difficulties with colleagues, speaking more in co-worker meetings, acquiring mediation skills.

3. Our vocational goals, for example: improving presentation skills, enhancing computer literacy, achieving more beautiful blackboard drawings, learning more about adolescence, improving time and project management skills.

Such development plans could also include courses or conferences we plan to attend in order to acquire particular insights and skills. These plans can be shared with a personnel committee, a care group or with a smaller group of colleagues; they can be reviewed annually as well as being looked at more briefly during the course of the year. A development plan of this kind can then be the link to a review of how well we are carrying out our particular roles or functions. It can encourage learning and growth.

Waldorf schools are profound learning communities for children, but often not such conscious learning communities for adults. Could every school establish a committee to foster community learning, asking each school group to assess their approach to learning and development? How does the individual teacher, how do the faculty as a group learn and develop? A learning committee or mandate group could organize an annual learning festival in which all the parts of the school community could share their successes and their learnings from the past year. Such a festival could be a joyous community celebration of the recently completed work.

A Culture of Service

In addition to becoming a learning culture, we can become a more conscious service culture in our institutions and communities. Part of becoming a service culture involves being more aware of our partners in our activities, whether as teachers, parents and children in a Waldorf school, or as co-workers, staff, residents and parents in a curative community. How does one make the nature of that partnership conscious? For me this is a central aspect of the service culture and an important part of community building. How do we actually do what many businesses do internally and externally? Who are our clients, how can we serve them better, and how do we explore with them what kind of job we're doing? Can we make it a virtue to learn from our partners more actively and to relate to them as true partners? Waldorf schools have developed a deeply caring culture of service toward children. How can that be extended to the relationship between adults and to the broader community in which the schools exist?

A student from Norway in the Waldorf School Administration and Community Development Program at Sunbridge College, Wolfgang Koetker applied a framework developed by Tim Collins in *Good to Great to Norwegian Waldorf Schools*. He asked what made some Waldorf schools great with healthy enrollment, good teachers and an excellent reputation, while others seemed to struggle over many years. He found that most important was excellence in teaching, but the second was the quality of service and success of partnership both within the school community and between the school and the community in which it was located. These excellent schools provided fairs and markets as well as events so that the school became a social and cultural center for their town or city, attracting people from far and wide. As he noted, good teachers attract more students, interest and resources which further attract excellent teachers and this when coupled with a strong sense of community service and good leadership builds a "flywheel of success" as described by Collins.[7]

An aspect of partnership is accountability. In most non-profit organizations it is the Board that is legally responsible, and it is the Board which represents the public interest. In collegial-run institutions with limited hierarchy, the question of accountability is critical. In

Waldorf schools, in what way are faculty accountable to Board and parents, and what accountability does the Board have and do the parents have? To spell out mutual expectations between Board, faculty, staff and parents based on a clear understanding of roles helps greatly in avoiding misunderstanding and conflict. This can be done in the school or parent handbook, containing more than a task description because it also needs to state how the parent association, the Board and the faculty are involved in key decisions such as tuition increases and other matters which involve all or most of the members of the school.

Part of developing a service culture is for each decision-making group to have clear criteria for evaluation and a transparent process of review. If the faculty have responsibility for all pedagogical decisions and the hiring, evaluation and dismissal of teachers, how is this done? The same applies to the Board. Is there a process for a Board audit or evaluation every year or two? Are criteria for Board membership made explicit and adhered to?

Underlying the notion of service is valuing competence. While volunteerism has its place in the childhood period of all initiatives, the need for professional skills and competence grows as the school enters maturity. Can all positions of responsibility, from the Christmas Fair Committee Chairperson to the hiring of the Kindergarten Assistant, be based on a clear understanding of the task and the skills and attitudes necessary to fill those positions? Volunteerism needs to be replaced by conscious selection of people and groups based on competence and a conscious review and thanking for all the work done on behalf of the whole. This is the essence of republican leadership and of a service culture, for it suggests we have a concern about quality and gratitude toward people who give so generously of their talents and time.

Building Community Consciously

I have described the need to deepen and broaden the community-building impulse of Waldorf education by developing a more conscious culture of leadership, learning and service. In developing a more conscious culture of learning and leadership, we deepen our connection to the spirit of the school and of Waldorf education by serving higher ideals. In becoming more conscious and skilled in meeting, we enliven the souls of our institutions, and in being more conscious of our partners, of those we serve and of how we serve them, we expand the culture of service. Developing a stronger culture of leadership, learning and service asks that we recommit ourselves to community building, to making our network of institutions healthier, more joyous places to live and work. This is the social challenge for us in the 21st century so that our schools can become beacons for the future. The powerful imagination of what it means to be human—carried in the Waldorf curriculum—needs to be brought more fully into our social architecture, into our practice, so that our communities can be places where people can more fully experience the light and blessings of the spirit.[8]

Chapter V Questions & Exercises:

I   Questions about Leadership:
- Who exercises what leadership responsibilities in our institution?
- How are leadership positions defined?
- How are leaders selected?
- What type of leadership do we want in different positions?
- What criteria and what process of selection do we require?
- Will individuals be given the time and support to carry out their functions?
- What education or training is provided for leadership?
- How will the exercise of leadership be reviewed?
- Can more experienced people mentor those in new leadership roles?
- Can we make the exercise of leadership a rewarding activity by thanking those who have accepted additional responsibility?

II   Questions about Service and Partnership:
Faculty:
- What are the main tasks of the faculty/school meeting?
- How does it serve the College and or the Leadership group:
  - Does it make decisions? In what areas?
  - Who does it need information from?
  - Who does it need to provide information to?
- Are there Upper School and Lower School Meetings?

- What are their decision-making responsibilities?
- To whom do they report?

College:
- Is there a College of Teachers or a Faculty Council?
- How is it chosen?
- To whom is it responsible?
- What decisions does it make?
- To whom are they communicated?

Board:
- What are the main responsibilities of the Board?
- How is it selected?
- Whom does it serve?
- What expectations, requests does it have of faculty and administration?
- What decisions does it make?
- To whom and how are they communicated?
- What are its main committees?
- How are they selected?
- To whom do they report?

Administration:
- What are the main administrative positions?
- Is there a school administrator?
- To whom does the administration report? How?
- Are administrators part of the faculty, College meetings?
- Are administrators part of the leadership group?

Parent Association:
- Is there a parent association?
- Who are members?
- What are its main tasks?
- How is it organized?
- How does it relate to the faculty and Board?
- How does it connect to the broader community?

III School and Community:
- What does the school offer to the local community?
- What services does the community offer the school?

- Does the school host a local market?
- Does it make its facilities open to others?
- Does it sponsor younger schools in the U.S. or abroad?
- Does it open its cultural events and festivals to others?

IV General Community Questions:
- How is the sense of belonging, of connectedness in the school community?
- How can this sense of connection be strengthened?
- What makes this Waldorf school unique?
- Consider three things that are virtues of the school.
- What can you do to help the school to blossom, to radiate and to flourish?

V Learning:
- Is there study and personal sharing and learning among the faculty?
- Is learning a focus in personnel policies and practices?
- Is there a review after faculty, Board and committee meetings? What is the mood of these reviews?
- Are there end-of-term or annual reviews of school functioning?
- Do the main decision-making groups meet once a year to ask what can we do to serve you and the school more effectively?
- Do you or could you imagine an annual learning festival for all adults in the school community?
- What might that look like?
- What can you do to strengthen your own learning and that of others in the school?

VI An Imagined Dialog among Friends:

Boomer Generation:

They don't work as hard as we do, nor are they as committed to anthroposophy. … You know when I listen to them and watch them, they have less energy than we do and are not really willing to sacrifice for the school. …Right. I have the same impression, and you know they want more time and money to honor their life choices. ... Yes, you know one younger colleague told me she needed her Pilates and yoga classes to be effective as a teacher. Imagine! ... I am just not sure that we can give them responsibility when they want to clarify all decision-making responsibilities and have a detailed job description. ... Can you imagine having a clear job description for being Faculty Chair? I do everything; even I don't know the full extent of my responsibilities. ...

Generation X:

Look at the sacrifices they make; I wouldn't want that... I have a family and two young children. Imagine being lead administrator and having to go to all those evening meetings, in addition to doing my normal work. ... Still, why don't they create more opportunities for us and help us understand how decisions are really made? ... You know, I often feel that the three of them decide and then bring the issue to the faculty meeting. ... Last week I was asked to be one of the faculty representatives on the Board, but I could not really find out what that entailed, how much time it required and whether I would get any comp time.

Endnotes

1. See Rudolf Steiner, *The Inner Aspect of the Social Question* (Rudolf Steiner Press, London, 1974). Also *Social and Anti-Social Forces in the Human Being* (Mercury Press, Spring Valley, NY, 1984) and "How Can the Soul Needs of the Time Be Met?" (Zurich, October 10, 1916) for descriptions of the rich spiritual perspective Rudolf Steiner brings to questions of community life.

2. Peter Block, *Stewardship: Choosing Service over Self-Interest* (Berrett-Koehler, San Francisco, 1993), p. 6. This is an excellent book for help in understanding the central aspect of leadership.

3. In Larry Spears, ed., *What Is Servant Leadership?* (Greenleaf Center, Indianapolis, 1998), p. 4. Also Robert Greenleaf, *The Servant as Leader* (Greenleaf Center, Indianapolis, 1978).

4. Ibid., pp. 5, 6. Also the excellent book by Stephen Covey, *Principle Centered Leadership* (Simon & Schuster, NY, 1990).

5. Op. cit., Steiner, "How Can the Soul Needs of the Time Be Met?"

6. For example, Peter Drucker, *Managing the Non-Profit Organization: Principles and Practices* (HarperCollins, NY, 1994).

7. Jim Collins, *Good to Great: Why Some Companies Make the Leap…and Others Don't* (HarperCollins, New York, 2001).

8. I have not dealt with the broader ethical and moral questions of leadership in this essay. For a look at these questions, see the insightful book by Torin Finser, *In Search of Ethical Leadership* (SteinerBooks, Great Barrington, MA, 2003).

This essay was adapted and updated from a talk given at a Leadership Symposium at Camphill Soltane, January 26–28, 1996. Its original title was: "Leadership in the Culture of Anthroposophical Organizations."

VI

Transformation and Renewal in Waldorf Schools

There is a kind of seeing which is also a kind of thinking...
the seeing of connections.

– Ray Monk

In this chapter I will briefly summarize the previously presented insights and perspectives on understanding Waldorf schools as organizations and then move on to describing important aspects of a systematic school renewal process. I will first describe general principles of organizational transformation, and then outline typical issues which provide an impetus for renewal, as well as aids for members of Waldorf school communities in initiating an institution-wide renewal process before reviewing useful strategies and approaches for initiating and shaping such a process.

We have seen that Waldorf schools and indeed all organizations are complex living systems, going through characteristic phases of development while also having a unique history and biography, much like we do as individuals. The Panjatai Waldorf school, located on the outskirts of Bangkok, recently graduated its first twelfth grade. It is still a pioneer Waldorf school, whereas Michael Hall, in England, is well established and has many traditions. It has been located on an old estate in Forest Row, Sussex, since the 1940s. Some Waldorf schools are urban in character, such as the City of Lakes Waldorf School in Minneapolis, whereas others are quite rural, Pine Hill in Wilton, New Hampshire, being one of many examples in the United States. While all Waldorf schools share the Waldorf curriculum and the rich image of child development which lies at the heart of the pedagogy, the teachers and staff of each school work with their children in a distinct manner, expressing the unique identity of each school and the culture and traditions of the country or region in which it is located.

The development of Waldorf schools takes place within a polarity of form and chaos. Periods of stability are followed by crises which are a spur to greater consciousness and to new forms and processes. It is tempting to think that we can rationally steer this process, to engineer change, but our own complexity and our experience with personal renewal and growth should be sufficient warning that what happens within ourselves and also within a school is difficult to perceive and not easy to guide. What we can do is learn to read what Allan Kaplan calls the "narrative thread," that subtle largely intangible need for change, the searching for new energy and for emerging possibilities, and to attempt to serve the school's renewal with all of our good will.[1] This reading of emerging possibilities is enhanced by seeing underlying connections and recognizing opportunities based on an increased understanding of institutional dynamics.

I Principles of School Development

There are a number of conditions or principles to school renewal and transformation which need to be understood and worked with in order to be able to help a school move forward with insight and consciousness, whether as a member of the school, a friend or a facilitator. These include:

1) The recognition that all Waldorf schools and indeed all organizations go through characteristic phases of development from birth to maturity. These phases have been described in some detail in the chapter on phases of school development (Chapter II), depicting a movement from the pioneer period, to the more rational consciousness of an administrative phase and to the more conscious, integrated or mature phase of a school's development.[2]

2) Institutional development and transformation involves growth as well as increasing differentiation in forms, functions and processes. Growth in the number of students and of faculty and staff is often the spur to the need for new structures and processes in the life of a school. When you have 140 children, 20 teachers and 6 staff, you cannot lead

and administer the school informally anymore. The need for greater clarity in policies and procedures as well as a less personal style of leadership leads to a crisis of confidence which then engenders the search for new forms.[3]

3) School development and transformation is irreversible and involves working with new organizational principles and a new consciousness. In the pioneer period, a relational intuitive consciousness supports informal structures and processes, whereas in the administrative phase, the clearer delegated forms need to be based on a more rational, administrative awareness. Once you have entered a new phase of development, you cannot go back to earlier principles and forms, although a new high school initiative will be in a pioneer period while the older kindergarten and grade school may have entered a more administrative phase, requiring the different parts of the school adjust to these differences.

4) School development is spurred by crises and challenges from either teachers or parents as people's experience of the school is at variance with the official narrative or espoused values. For example, if collegial partnership forms and quality education are espoused values but hiring and evaluation processes are not clear and personality based leadership predominates, then the perceived discrepancy will lead to dissatisfaction and the loss of students until change occurs.

5) The more mature an organization is, the more conscious the renewal and transformation process needs to be and the harder it becomes to achieve desired change. The development of the school from its pioneer period into a more rational administrative phase of development happens more or less naturally but often not without struggle. Further developments are more difficult as mature organizations have a proven record of success and have developed many traditions so that renewal requires the sacrifice of what has worked in the past. Another way of putting this is to say that the larger, older, and more complex a school is, the greater the resistance to change.

In addition to the phases of organization development, I have found two other frameworks useful in identifying the need and direction for change in the life of the school. One of these is the model of the Three Dialogs, described in Chapters II and III.[4] In the same way that our health is dependent on 1) a dialog with the spirit, with our values and purpose in life; 2) a dialog with people: family, friends and colleagues; and 3) a dialog with the earth, with our body, our work and with physical activity in general, so too is a school's health. Questions one can ask of any Waldorf school include:

Dialog with the Spirit:

- What is the mission and purpose of the school?
- Are the school's values and policies aligned with this mission?
- How are the vision and mission kept alive?
- Is excellence in teaching a priority and how does this manifest in the life of the school?
- How does the school foster a dialog with the spirit? For example, is child study done and is it alive? Are the festivals rich and uplifting? Does the College of Teachers work with a pedagogical study and together on questions of inner development?

Dialog with People:

- What is the quality and mood of relationships between teachers, teachers and children, and teachers and parents?
- What is the quality of meetings, of all-school gatherings and of parent evenings?
- How are the school's relationships with the surrounding community and with other schools in the region?
- How can trust and listening be improved?
- What shifts in attitudes, skills and behavior are needed to improve the soul mood and quality of the human dialog?

Dialog with the Earth:

- How is the school governed and administered?
- What are the leadership structures and principles?
- What is the health of the finances?

- Are the building and grounds beautiful and clean?
- What can be done to improve the school's dialog with the earth, with its work processes and its physical home?

By using these questions, members of the school community can both explore present strengths and weaknesses as well as determine the direction of future change.

A third and complementary diagnostic perspective is looking at the seven functions of organizational health called "Jacob's Ladder" by many of my former colleagues at MIRA, an organizational development consultancy group with its base in Europe. The seven functions referred to are most relevant to schools already in an administrative or mature phase of development.

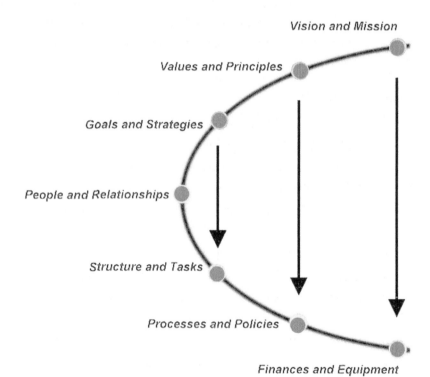

The questions to consider with each dimension of school life are:

- How conscious is the school about its vision or about its governance structure and decision-making process?
- To what degree are the activities and processes or relationships commonly understood and supported?
- Where are there gaps in understanding or support?
- What can be done to strengthen one or the other dimension of the school's life?

The framework is useful primarily in sharpening awareness and doing a self-diagnosis of what is in place and what needs attention. It is a supplement to the phase model and the three dialogs as a way of thinking and talking about the school as a living organism.[5]

II Renewal Issues

Personality Conflicts:

There are a number of critical issues in Waldorf schools which often trigger crises and which, if met consciously, lead to renewal and transformation. One of these is personal conflicts between teachers due to personality differences and the struggle for power and influence. I have experienced working in Waldorf schools where the faculty was so polarized that some faculty members no longer spoke to each other while others felt helpless and disempowered. Such conflicts are exascerbated in partnership structures with limited hierarchy and can affect the quality of teaching as well as undermine decision making. They also have a way of spilling over into the broader community, leading to unhappy children and parents, and they tend to pollute the soul space of the school, as thoughts and feelings are real. Even when unstated, they have profound effects on the attitudes, feelings and behavior of all school members.

The same applies to conflicts between teachers and parents which are often caused by lack of clarity about teacher hiring, mentoring, evaluation and dismissal or unclear governance structures. In such situations, outside facilitation is often critical because everyone within the school is suspect and is thought to have taken sides.

Teacher Hiring, Mentoring, Evaluation and Dismissal:

The issue of excellence in teaching and the quality of teacher hiring, mentoring, evaluation and firing is one of the most challenging issues facing Waldorf schools, since the collegial partnership forms of Waldorf education make objectivity and due process difficult. When parents sense that the quality of the education is excellent and their children's needs are being met, they are happy. However when teacher hiring, mentoring and evaluation policies and processes are not clear and when excellence in the classroom is not the schools number one priority, then parents grow anxious and begin looking at all aspects of the school's life.

The situation is made more difficult by teachers not responding to inquiries or saying the faculty knows best. I have frequently experienced cases in Waldorf schools where hiring was not based on the quality of the applicant, where references were not checked and where trained and experienced teachers were not hired and untrained and inexperienced teachers were, based on their special relationship with one or more faculty or staff. The opposite can also be true where trained and experienced but now unsuccessful teachers are recycled through the Waldorf School Movement because the new school was not careful enough in checking references, assuming that if there were problems they would have heard.

There is also the connected issue of terminating class teachers who are not working out. Given the sensitivity of the issues and their confidential nature, parents may feel that "their teacher" has been victimized. The parents then often become polarized and question the school's leadership and decision making. To answer these questions it is important to make sure that assuring excellence in teaching is the faculty's number one priority and that hiring, mentoring and evaluation policies are clear, transparent to everyone and adhered to by the personnel committee. More mature and successful Waldorf schools have developed clear hiring mentoring and evaluation policies and processes, and ASWNA has sample policies and "Best Practices" available.

This leads me to make an observation based on years of sometimes painful experience working with Waldorf schools. When the spiritual and pedagogical life of a school is not strong, then social life and relationships suffer, which in turn leads to a breakdown of working structures and agreements. There is a cascade of disfunctionality when people can no longer trust their mutual commitment to the ideals and values of the education because then personality differences begin to appear insurmountable and no true working agreements can be found. I once worked with a Canadian Waldorf school in which the commitment to Waldorf education was weak and where the differences about whether Waldorf schools were Christian schools or not became so severe that the faculty could not make important decisions about the school's future. Working on relationships and communication or changing the governance structure under these circumstances does not help. What is needed then is a recommitment to the principles of Waldorf education, a deepening of child and pedagogical study and mutual work on questions of inner development.

Unclarity or Disagreements on Governance Structure and Principles:

Most organizations, including most schools, are organized hierarchically, and power is defined in terms of leaders and subordinates. As we have seen, Rudolf Steiner intended the faculty of the first Waldorf school to work together as colleagues and to delegate responsibilities as appropriate. Parents, in most cases coming from more conventional organizational cultures, often have difficulty understanding Waldorf school culture and forms and question the school's leadership and decision making. This makes it incumbent on Waldorf schools to not only be clear about their governance and leadership forms but articulate the rationale behind them.

As we saw in Chapter III, most Waldorf schools in the United States have one of three basic governance forms: faculty-run schools; partnership forms in which a strong faculty and a strong Board are supported by a capable administration; and Board-run schools in which the Board appoints a school head. In practice there are of course many variations to these three basic approaches. While it is my contention that colleagial partnership forms are in the long run the most effective way of governing and still adhering to the basic social insights of Rudolf Steiner, there are examples of successful Waldorf schools using variations of each of these three basic governance models.

What is most important is that schools clearly articulate the principles and forms of their governance structures, who the main faculty decision-making groups are, and what their responsibilities, membership and reporting relationships are. The same need for clarity applies to the Board and its committees, the administration and the parent association.

When decision-making responsibilities are clear and positions filled on the basis of competency, then in most cases parents will accept and support the governance principles and forms being worked with. When they do not, it is usually because the forms and principles are not clear, or leadership positions are not filled on the basis of competence, or when one of two mistaken assumptions is made about Waldorf school governance. The first of these is that because Waldorf schools seem to embody an alternative approach to education, then they need to be democracies in which everyone—parents, teachers and staff—has an equal voice in decision making. This is not and cannot be the case given the teacher's responsibility for providing an excellent Waldorf education. Rather the school is organized on republican principles of delegated responsibilities, based on insight, experience and competence as we saw in Chapter III. The second assumption can be equally destructive, namely that efficient and hierarchical management criteria are the most important values to embody in the school's governance. Such values have their place in administration, but when applied to the school as whole, they lead to undermining the dialog culture of Waldorf education and the crucial involvement of teachers in many aspects of the school's management.

Leadership:

As was noted in the essay on leadership, learning and service in Waldorf schools, there is a clear need for Waldorf schools to have an imagination for leadership in keeping with the values and principles of the education. Examples of such a service-oriented and spirit-filled imagination of leadership can be found in the work of Robert Greenleaf on *Servant Leadership* and of Peter Block.[6] Developing an imagination of leadership and grounding it through clear policies and procedures on leadership positions, selection, evaluation and support is critical to the future of many Waldorf schools as an older, more sacrificial generation of Baby Boomers (born between 1943–1960) is retiring, but often reluctantly, in part because of limited financial means.[7] The Waldorf movement and younger parents need to recognize that the the growth and success of Waldorf education was built on the energy and often the financial sacrifice of an older generation of founding teachers. Equally the older generation can acknowledge that younger teachers of Generation X (born between 1961–1981) need their support, encouragement and understanding in order to step into positions of responsibility. Waldorf schools have nothing to lose and much to gain from an open discussion of leadership questions. It is one of the issues which, if addressed consciously, can further the development of each school and of the Waldorf Movement as a whole.

The Delegation of Responsibility and the Creation of Committees and Mandate Groups:

In many growing Waldorf schools there are complaints about endless meetings, ineffective decision making and poor leadership. In my experience these complaints have three main causes. The first is limited social and group skills so that meetings are not led and facilitated well and, because of time pressures, not reviewed, so that common learning and development do not take place.[8] A second has already been mentioned, namely the lack of clarity about committee mandates, responsibilities and reporting relationships. This leads to the third cause, namely the undermining of committee or mandate group decision making by a faculty, Board or administration loath to delegate its responsibilities. The lack of delegation and the often endless discussion of issues in the full faculty or Board meeting is not only inefficient but drives many teachers and active parents away from involvement in the running of the school.

Poor Finances and Limited Financial Awareness:

Money can be seen as the lifeblood of the school. It supports the vibrancy of the teaching, the rich community life and the quality of the buildings and grounds. In most American Waldorf schools, the main sources of financial support are tuitions and gifts, with the exception of the Waldorf-inspired charter schools. Much comes to expression in the health or lack of health in the school's finances, not only the level of enrollment but clearly the quality of teaching and the prevailing mood in parent-teacher relations. I once worked with a school which consistently struggled with enrollment and finances. Teachers complained about low salaries and the general lack of support from parents. As enrollment continued to drop, the faculty finally had to confront their own negligence in not dealing with some poor quality teaching in the kindergarten and in three of its six grades.

Faculty and parents need to understand that the school's finances are a mirror, a reflection of what is happening in other aspects of the school's life. This means that financial administration needs to be clear, accurate and transparent and that faculty, Board and parents need to be given periodic updates on the school's projected and actual budget. Not everyone needs to be an accountant or a financial wizard, but all members of the school community should be interested in understanding the basic aspects of the school's financial situation.

Quite recently a friend and former student of mine, Wolfgang Koetker did a study of Waldorf education in Norway. In particular he was interested in the question of why some Waldorf schools had an excellent reputation over many years, while others were seen as mediocre and a few suffered from continuous struggles. He applied the insights of Jim Collins' best-selling book *Good to Great* to a number of schools, doing both case studies and extensive interviews.[9] He came to the conclusion that excellent Waldorf schools apply the lessons of what Collins called the "hedgehog concept" after the Aesop's fable of the Hedgehog and the Fox. While the fox was intelligent, fast and adventurous, he invariably hurt his nose when he attempted to devour the hedgehog, for the hedgehog did a few things very well, including curling up in a ball to protect himself with his spikes. For schools paying attention to the basics this means having a passion for the quality of Waldorf education, understanding what the school can uniquely contribute to the larger community as well as to the families it serves and, thirdly, deeply understanding the resource and financial base of the school.

What Koetker found was that excellent Waldorf schools in Norway focus strongly on the quality of teaching in the classroom, and have a long-term and living commitment to the principles and values of Waldorf education (mission). They also provide a strong festival and community life as well as unique programs for the surrounding community, whether a Saturday market, a concert series, or a gardening and farm-based program for adolescents. Not surprisingly, they also have a transparent and community-based understanding of the school's finances and a good relationship with the government representatives who provided eighty to ninety percent of the school's revenue.[10] Those Waldorf schools with mediocre or poor reputations did not do nearly so well in these areas, suffering higher teacher turnover, lower enrollment and a less secure financial base.

The schools with an excellent reputation over time have also experienced what Collins calls the "flywheel of success," alluding to the heavy flywheel in marine diesel engines, which once you get it going, it goes on steadily forever. The principle is simple: Excellent teachers attract more students, leading to full enrollment and better finances which in turn enhances the reputation of the school, which in turn leads to attracting better teachers, and so on.[11]

Collins' hedgehog concept is very similar in nature to the principles of the three dialogs, described previously: A creative dialog with the mission and spiritual values of the school and an open and effective dialog among the constituents of the school will enhance the physical and financial resources available to the school.

III Aids in School Renewal

School development is an extra.

Systematic school renewal requires an extra effort and a considerable commitment of time by the members of the school community. The effort required is in addition to the school's meeting its ongoing educational and social obligations. It is therefore best not to attempt a strategic planning process, a major overhaul of administration or a capital campaign during a time of crisis, as the number of meetings and the amount of time required to involve all relevant stakeholders and to assure a successful outcome is substantial.

Assume that every member of the school community has access to the truth and in principle knows the direction for future change.

We may be tempted to think that only people in leadership positions really understand what is happening in a school, but in my experience the socially-oriented receptionist or the sympathetic bookkeeper may know as much about the range of issues facing the school as the Faculty Chair. When looking at present strengths and weaknesses or exploring future possibilities, include all members of the school community; everyone has insights of value. In finalizing future plans or steps the faculty, College of Teachers, Board or the Long Range Planning Committee will rightly make final decisions, but it is advisable to remember that new developments are most successful when everyone owns the changes being planned.

Attend to your school, learn its biography and history; let it tell you what is needed.

As a young academic teaching at MIT during the time of the Vietnam War, I was horrified and angry at the ways in which my institution and indeed my department were complicit in the war effort. I protested and demonstrated with the students. However it was only when I developed an interest in the history of MIT and began talking to students and colleagues and could see the many positive things that the university provided to the local community, to the development of modern science and to our society at large, that I was given an opportunity to act. When my attitude shifted, I was asked to teach a course on U.S. Foreign Policy to undergraduates and was asked to join a Technology and Culture Committee which had the opportunity of sponsoring research seminars and conferences with academics from around the world. This of course did not change the funding links between the Department of Defense and the university, but it did allow me, working with others, to bring other perspectives and viewpoints into the dialog with students and faculty.

I had a similar experience while facilitating a number of retreats for the Association for Research and Enlightenment (ARE) in Virginia Beach. Through studying its biography and its programs and membership, I realized that the organization kept only ten percent of its new members for more than two years. Although the membership was large—about 50,000 people in the late 1980s—the core membership was 10,000, and the rest had been recruited through clever advertising. I was then able to ask the Board and the Leadership Group whether they wished to be a door to new age spirituality or to provide a home with different rooms. This turned out to be a very important question which led the organization to further clarify its mission and purpose.

The study of a school's biography gives one insight into underlying themes and patterns which are deeply embedded in the school's history. The Kimberton Waldorf School was started in the middle of World War II with some of the original German Waldorf teachers from the Stuttgart school, but it also had a popular junior high school teacher, who knew nothing about Waldorf education, as the school's first headmistress. Throughout much of the school's early history it struggled with the question of whether it was to be a mainline prep school or a committed Waldorf school.

Every significant school renewal process should rest on a deep and shared understanding of its biography and history. A new and actively willed future is based on the reality of what was created in the past.

Develop a common language and conceptual framework for talking about the school.

I have suggested different frameworks for talking about the process of school development: the phases of school development, the three dialogs and Collins' hedgehog concept. To this I would add a concept for looking at different dimensions of the school's life in order to understand present strengths and weaknesses. Known as "Jacobs Ladder," it was originally developed by the Netherlands Pedagogical Institute (NPI)in Holland and adapted by MIRA: Companions in Development, an international organizational development institute. (See diagram on page 120.)

Recognize that school development and renewal requires a systematic process with a sequence of steps and will take from a few months to a year.

School renewal, if it is to develop the whole school as a living system, needs to be supported by the leadership of the school and in particular by the Board and faculty. It also needs to be a planned and systematic process with sequential steps and outcomes, some of which are described in the next section of this essay and in the exercises at the end of this chapter.

Have a learning focus in all-school development activities.

If school excellence is the goal of all Waldorf schools, then any effort to renew and develop a school needs to be based on a commitment to organizational learning. What is working well and what needs improvement? How do we make those changes which will move us toward the goal of school excellence in all areas of the school's life? This needs to be the basic learning orientation of the school community whether in areas of administration, group and committee meetings, quality of teaching or the fostering of community life. Such a learning orientation means learning from experience or action-learning previously described and should be practiced by the adult members of the school in an ongoing way, not only in a time of crisis or struggle. The virtue of a learning focus is that it leads the members of the school community into periodic reflection on what they can do to improve the school's functioning as well as avoiding the all-too-human tendency to look for individuals or groups to blame for existing shortcomings.

Work with both the good spirit and with the shadow of the school.

Each school has a unique spirit, a being who accompanies the school on its developmental journey much like the good spirit or angel of the child. But there is also another and darker spiritual dimension to all institutional life. It is the realm of the double or the shadow side of all human and social life, created out of our unconscious habits, our untransformed sides, our pettinesses and our lower drives for power, approval and wealth. This is as true for institutions and for countries as it is for us as individuals. The United States has traditionally disguised its foreign policy interests under the rationale of supporting democracy and freedom while often promoting authoritarian regimes which seem to be more congenial allies than democratic governments. Some Waldorf schools make a virtue of using anthroposophical or Waldorf orthodoxy as a defense against looking at important issues raised by parents or friends regarding the quality of the education or the need to rethink the high school language curriculum.

A way of working with the good spirit of the school is to reflect on the qualities which make this particular Waldorf school unique and to draw or imagine the qualities which the members of the school community admire and feel good about. This may be the school's commitment to diversity and accessibility, or the atmosphere of mutual support among the teachers, or the strong and lively pedagogical study at the school. Working with the good spirit of the school refers to co-creating with the spirit and is described in some detail in Chapter VIII. It can find expression in having the College of Teachers or the Board ask for guidance, working with verses such as the America or Threefold Verse or strengthening a meditative awareness that we are working together with a spiritual being which wishes to support our work as much as we wish to have such support. This type of awareness is of particular importance in a school renewal process as we are recreating the physical and soul space which we and the good spirit of the school will jointly share.

Becoming aware of the school's double can be achieved by exploring those issues which repeatedly block the school's development and which are difficult, and often impossible, to talk about openly. I worked with one school where a very difficult conflict many years ago was still not able to be discussed even though none of the parties involved were still at the school. Another double issue which I am aware of in some schools is when the private lives of teachers and parents become the main topic of the rumor mill, as families are torn apart through multiple shifting partnerships. Another kind of issue which can be experienced in some Waldorf schools is the hidden exercise of power, of cliques among the faculty and/or Board, which cannot be discussed or overcome. What we can see in each of these situations is that human frailties become the basis of negative spiritual energies which block the strong positive working of our own good spirit as well as the good spirit of the school. The invitation in all Waldorf school communities is to be aware that we are beheld, that we are co-creating with human and spiritual beings, and that we want to create the best educational, moral and spiritual environment for our children.

IV Approaches and Strategies of Renewal

There are many approaches and strategies to school and organizational development. I will describe those which I have found to be most helpful in working with Waldorf schools and other cultural and social organizations. A distinction needs to be made between approaches and strategies which focus on a particular issue or need, such as creating a better, more transparent accounting system or on improving the communication and group facilitation skills of faculty and staff, and a whole-system change which involves changes in values, relationships, structures and processes. I have worked with some Waldorf schools where relatively small changes or specific approaches to particular issues have produced significant benefits. Providing ongoing training in communication, facilitation and conflict resolution skills has benefited many Waldorf schools, saving time and leading to more productive meetings. Restructuring, such as appointing an Administrative Director to provide supervision to an administration of six people previously working as equals, can bring more clarity and accountability to the school's administration.

In one Waldorf school, clarifying committee mandates and mutual reporting relationships brought about a significant improvement in decision making and overall functioning, while in another changing the school's name to include "Waldorf" served to focus the school's intention and strengthen the faculty's commitment. In still another Waldorf school characterized by a history of conflict among faculty members, simply spelling out the school's expectations of a faculty member's time, meeting commitments and acceptable behavior in the annual employment contract made a big difference, since it created a more equal and conscious framework for dialog and assessment. In another school, developing job descriptions for leadership positions and developing clear hiring and evaluation policies for those positions improved functioning significantly. If the school is aware of a particular issue or question which has created problems over a period of time, a problem-solving orientation is appropriate and can achieve results. A survey of the school community every two to three years, exploring existing strengths and weaknesses, is a good way to identify specific issues to work on, as is an all-school or an administrative audit done by an outside advisor or facilitator every four or five years.

In describing approaches to whole-system development and transformation, I will describe briefly four different but interconnected orientations. They have similarities and each assumes the support of the school leadership and the participation of the school community's members in the renewal process. They are ways of conceptualizing and sequencing the school's renewal process.

Appreciative Inquiry: David Cooperrider and colleagues have developed an approach to institutional renewal focusing on strengthening what is energizing, innovative and motivating about the organization. As opposed to concentrating on weaknesses or problems to be solved, their methodology looks at the positive achievements and traditions of an institution and makes this the source of renewal. At the heart of this renewal process is the appreciative inquiry interview in which members of the school are asked questions such as:

1. Please describe a high point for you working in this organization.

2. Tell us what you value about yourself, about your colleagues and about your school.

3. What are the core qualities which make the school or organization what it is today?

4. What three wishes or dreams do you have for improving the health and vitality of your school?

Based on this search for the positive and unique through appreciative inquiry interviews with many people in the organization, a process is designed for people to share their Discoveries about their school, then they share their Dreams about what might be, before turning to Designing and Constructing plans and approaches for renewal. Finally the question of how to empower, create and sustain change is called Destiny.[12]

Theory U and Presencing: Because of its strong future orientation, similar to that of Appreciative Inquiry, I would next mention Klaus Otto Scharmer's Theory U. Scharmer encourages us to "learn from a future that has not yet happened and from continually discovering our part in bringing that future to pass." He describes a sevenfold process from looking at patterns of the past to seeing the present with new eyes, to sensing the school's environment and needs and then to connecting to the source, to the being of the organization as well as to our own higher intentions. From here it becomes a question of crystallizing, prototyping and creating the needed future. These steps are described briefly in the diagram below and can be worked on over a number of meetings and retreats by all or some of the institution's members.

DOWNLOADING   PERFORMING
(working from patterns of the past)   (creating new practices)

(OPEN MIND)

SEEING ANEW   PROTOTYPING
(having an open mind)   (co-creating possibilities)

(OPEN HEART)

SENSING   CRYSTALLIZING
(achieving a common awareness)   (visions and intentions)

(OPEN WILL)

PRESENCING
(connecting to the source)

The U-Process involves a deepening of commitment and intention on the part of all participants to serve the school and the future through developing an open mind and an open heart and listening and attending to what is wanted. It is both a social process and a spiritual practice to suspend all preconceptions and personal interests to serve the whole.[13] (See Luigi Morelli, *A Revolution of Hope*, pp. 244–252, for an excellent short summary of Theory U and possibilities for implementation.)

Future Search and Search Conferences: Based on the foundational work of Eric Trist and Fred Emery and adapted by Marvin Weisbord and Sandra Janoff, Future Search Conferences involve a three- or four-day-process of creating a commonly shared vision of the future and developing an action plan for achieving it. Typically such a process involves six distinct phases: 1) world trends and the context for the organization, 2) trends and developments which affect the school or institution, 3) the biography and evolution of the school, 4) creating a vision for the future, 5) developing strategies and plans and 6) gaining commitment and developing an action plan.[14] (A good summary and daily schedule for a future search conference is provided by Cornelis Pieterse in *Empowerment in Organizations*, pp. 99–112.)

Vision in Action: This is a long-term planning and visioning process that typically takes from six months to a year and is externally facilitated. It is based on work done by the author with colleagues in Europe and worked with by him in many Waldorf schools in the United States and elsewhere since the early 1980s. Typically there are three all-school retreats: the first to review the biography and the present strengths and weaknesses of the school; the second, to develop a vision for the school, an imagination of future possibilities and clarifying or modifying the mission statement; and the third, to review and fine-tune the long-term plan. The process is normally carried by a long-term planning group consisting of teachers, parents and Board members. It is described in some detail at the end of this essay and is summarized in the chart on the next page. A significant difference from other approaches is that the process involves a clear articulation of values regarding governance and community life as well as the formulation of a clear educational philosophy.[15] (See Christopher Schaefer and Tÿno Voors, *Vision in Action*, pp. 163–177, for a more detailed description, parts of which are contained in the exercises at the end of this chapter.)

Which of these approaches is worked with depends on the school's circumstances and the facilitator hired to assist the school with its renewal process. Irrespective of the approach and process chosen, it is important to remember that all institutional renewal is uncomfortable and generates resistance to change. This resistance is expressed through doubt in our thinking life: "We tried a planning process six years ago and it didn't work." "Outside facilitators are expensive and they do not understand our culture." In our feeling life the resistance expresses itself through dislike and irritation, and in our will life through fear about the loss of a position or a change in our responsibilities. These resistances

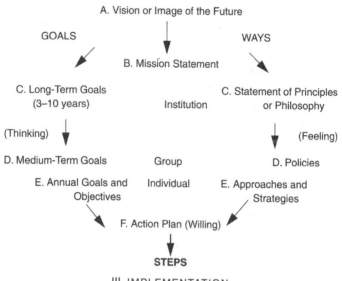

I. PREPARATION
1. Biography
2. Strengths and Weaknesses
3. Assumptions about the Future

II. LONG-TERM PLANNING (0–20 years)

A. Vision or Image of the Future

GOALS   WAYS

B. Mission Statement

C. Long-Term Goals   C. Statement of Principles
(3–10 years)   Institution   or Philosophy

(Thinking)   (Feeling)

D. Medium-Term Goals   Group   D. Policies

E. Annual Goals and   Individual   E. Approaches and
Objectives   Strategies

F. Action Plan (Willing)

STEPS

III. IMPLEMENTATION

IV. EVALUATION, REFORMULATION

have legitimacy and need to be honored by keeping the following principles in mind when working with strategies and processes of school renewal:

- Help the members of the school community own the issues and problems the school faces.

- Involve everyone in finding future directions and possibilities.

- Take small and medium steps toward the future and review results.

- Do not draw out the renewal process for more than a year.

- Celebrate successes, and

- Attempt to work with the good spirit of the school.

In ending it is good to remember that social processes are not linear and that our efforts to renew and transform our schools and institutions will often have unanticipated consequences since community development is more of an art than a science and we are just beginning to learn what it means to create and recreate a healthy social world.[16]

Chapter VI Exercises:

I. Preparation

While it may be tempting to think that we can fashion a new self or a new organization by planning, to do so is clearly not possible. An understanding of the organization's history and of its present strengths and weaknesses is therefore an essential foundation.

1. Biographical Review:

- When was the college, company, clinic, school or store started?

- By whom was it started?

- What was the first set of critical questions?

- What has been the historical development?

- What are the themes, patterns and relationships in the initiative's biography?

For example, the Association for Research and Enlightenment (A.R.E.), in Virginia Beach, has been led and guided by three generations of Cayces, first Edgar Cayce, then Hugh Lynn Cayce, and then Charles Thomas Cayce, each giving a particular stamp to the organization. The New York Open Center was based on a close working relationship between Ralph White, an experienced program person, and a New York lawyer, Walter Beebe, whose vision, drive, connections and administrative capacities helped this initiative get off the ground. The Asten group, in the paper-forming fabric business, has, through generations, been guided by a partnership between a sales personality and a technical engineering person. In each case these personalities and relationships have played an important role in the institution's history.

The biography needs to be more than a superficial narrative, and people need to be given the opportunity to comment and to contribute.

However, it is often best to give an individual or a small group the task to pull this together in draft form.

2. Assessment of Current Strengths and Weaknesses:

What are the present strengths and weaknesses of the school, store, clinic, association or company?

- How well is it organized?

- What are its finances like?

- What are the present organizational forms? Which work and which don't?

- What about the quality of relationships between people within the organization and also with customers, clients or parents?

- What phase of development is the organization in?

- How is the dialogue with the spirit, with people and with the earth?

- What issues would coworkers and clients like to see addressed?

In doing such a self-assessment, it is often good to prepare a questionnaire for people both outside and within the organization, following up with selected interviews. A review and sharing can then take place in a conference with coworkers and others.

3. Assumptions about the Future

As an additional part of the preparation it is important to make some assumptions about the future—about the kind of development that will affect the environment of the organization. Will the town and the community still need a private school? What are the population and income projections for the county? Will the future bring a still greater interest in natural foods and alternative medicine? This last question is critical for the health food industry and for alternative approaches to healing. For each initiative there are a number of quite specific questions the answers to which will affect its future directly and some more general assumptions that will need to be discussed. While some research will help, often we need to make educated guesses about the likely interest in our service or product and about the probable evolution of the economy.

Having completed these steps, the organization can enter planning for the future with a shared sense of identity. Without such a basis, planning can become an illusion.

II. Long-Term Planning

A. Vision or Image of the Future

A vision of the future is an imagination of what we would like the organization to be ten to twenty years from now. It needs to contain a dream that can motivate and guide, like a star that gives light to navigate by. This is not an easy thing to develop, for it is not a question of describing more buildings, students or products, but rather a combination of qualities and activities that form a living whole.

The Door, a New York center for adolescents, had a vision of a totally integrated set of services for young people in need: counseling, nutrition, an alternative high school, job training, athletic and exercise programs, and a referral service all in one location. When the New York Open Center started in downtown Manhattan, it had a vision of being a center for spirituality, embracing both Eastern and Western esoteric traditions. Henry Ford had a vision of designing and producing an automobile so efficiently and paying such good wages that everyone could afford a Model T. A vision, if it addresses a real need in the world, has a way of drawing around it the people and resources needed to make it happen.

B. The Mission Statement

As Peter Drucker pointed out in his book Managing the Non-Profit Organization, "A mission statement has to focus on what the institution really tries to do."[17] It should not be too long or too complicated, and it should have implications for the operation of the organization. Waldorf schools often state that their mission is to educate for freedom. This then needs some elaboration so that the teachers, parents and friends know what is meant and know what their contribution to the mission can be. The A.R.E., the spiritual movement founded by Edgar Cayce, has the mission of making manifest the love of God and man through Awakening, Educating, Applying, Sharing and Serving.[18] The mission of the New York Open Center is to be "a focal point for holistic thinking and practice in the heart of New York City."[19] Sears Roebuck used to have the mission of being the informed and responsible buyer for the American family, which was an incredibly successful approach to retailing until a few years ago. A consultancy group of which I am part has the mission of helping individuals, groups and institutions take their next steps in development.

There are a number of important factors regarding the mission of an organization:

- Keeping it simple
- Doing what you already do better
- Really making a difference—responding to a real need
- Believing in what you are doing
- Trying to make it live in all of your activity

C. A Statement of Philosophy or Principles

If we now return to the diagram on long-term planning, two paths are indicated, a path of goals and another of ways or means. I have usually preferred to move from the mission statement of philosophy or values, as the mission quite naturally leads to these kinds of reflections. The W.K. Kellogg Foundation has a philosophical commitment to life-long open learning, supporting the education of its employees.[20] Mabou, a successful small department store in Saratoga Springs, New York, had a philosophy of treating the customer as a guest and the salesperson as a host. It also worked at allowing each employee to become what they were capable of being. The Asten Group has the philosophy of creating a true sense of community in the company.

Statements of principles should also include statements about how the organization is structured and the quality of relationships.

D. A Statement of Long-Term Goals (3–10 years)

The statement of long-term goals needs to articulate the major goals of the organization over a longer period of time, anywhere from three to ten years. In their last long-term plan (1980–1990) the A.R.E. had the goals of becoming a major publisher and distributor of quality books related to psychic research and of increasing their membership sevenfold. The goals of Shining Mountain Waldorf School in Boulder, Colorado, included starting a high school and building an arts complex and auditorium. The New York Open Center had goals of building an active board and a number of larger courses and programs connected to professional training.

A statement of long-term goals should not be too complex and should contain clear priorities.

E. Medium-Term Goals, Approaches and Policies

Medium-term goals should consist of a breakdown of major goals into distinct areas and contain statements about how these goals are to be achieved. These "how" statements reflect strategies and values, and an assessment of what activities are likely to be most successful in achieving the desired goals within the value framework of the organization. They can include extending the range of products or services, raising salaries or improving profitability. Goal areas and policies naturally extend the mission statement and philosophy of the institution. In the case of a high school, policies about teacher hiring, financial aid, discipline and salaries indicate how the institution will carry out its day-to-day activities within the context of preferred values. For companies, policies on quality, assessment, customer relations and decision-making have the same impact. If policies are not articulated and do not reflect the statement of principles or philosophy of the organization, then that philosophy becomes an unread Bible sitting in the lowest desk drawer of a few individuals.

F. Annual Goals, Objectives, Approaches and the Action Plan

Annual goals, objectives and approaches describe what you hope to achieve in the next year or two. If the New York Open Center wants to extend the range of longer courses and seminars, how many of these and in what areas in year 1, 2, 3, 4? If the Community Supported Agriculture project has the long-range goal of hiring two gardeners and having 250 supporting families, then what has to be achieved in year 1, in year 2, and how? If Sunbridge College wishes to become a University of the Spirit, what kind of programs and activities are needed to help it move from being predominately a teacher training center?

The articulation of annual goals, objectives and approaches already describes much of the action plan, which then spells out who will do what and how results will be reviewed.

III. The Planning Process and the Implementation of the Long-Range Plan

Before turning to the question of implementation, I want to refer to a number of essential factors that affect the success or failure of the planning process and the plan itself.

The planning process should not take too long, or the organization will experience it as an excessive burden. In my experience, it should not take longer than a year. In addition, the process needs to be carried as a high priority by the key individuals or leadership group of the organization. If it is not carried as a high priority, it is experienced as hollow or as a diversion by the rest of the organization. A connected issue is the degree to which the leadership group and the organization as a whole model, believe in, and attempt to embody the values and priorities expressed in the plan. The phrase "walk the talk" contains wisdom. Lastly, and I think extremely important, is the degree to which the whole organization shares the vision, mission and plan. The more it is owned, the greater the chance of success. Therefore the process of participation and involvement is as important as the documents produced. Opportunities for involvement, comment and discussion should be given to all members of the organizational family—including support staff. How this is done depends on the size and nature of the organization.[21]

The question of implementation is dependent upon whether the plan is fully integrated as an ongoing basis into the life of the institution or is being carried only by a small planning group with limited authority. Is it reviewed regularly by the Board and the main decision-making groups? Is it integrated into the discussion and decisions of committees or departments?

IV. Evaluation and Reformulating

For the long-term plan to have meaning, it must contain goals and activities that are capable of being reviewed. Did we achieve what we wanted in the areas of services, programs and finances and in the time anticipated? If not, were we unrealistic to begin with? Did we set the wrong priorities or not free enough people to work on them? If the plan is for five years or even three, then a quarterly review of activities and progress needs to be done and periodic adjustments made in goals and timetable.

As a plan has validity only for a limited period of time—between three to ten years—and as organizations and people change, a new planning process will be periodically needed to renew the focus and commitment of the initiative to re-create and redirect the organization.

Hygiene of the Organizational Soul

A Consensus Vision Process That Generates Enthusiasm and Commitment*

by Jean Yeager —August 1993

The Case: The Baltimore Waldorf School
Several purposes were clearly articulated by the president and vice-president of the Board and by the faculty chair:

1. The school had recently been restructured by a joint faculty/ Board/ parent committee. The recent past had been stressful for the school community. It was felt that it was important to reconnect as a community.

2. There were pressures for change in many places: location and site constraints; a high school program was being discussed; creating multicultural programs and programs for children with special needs were requested; and many more issues had been discussed and debated. There were multiple visions for the future being formed. The Board and faculty felt the need to reach a consensus about the priorities for the future. Originally it was thought that by the end of this meeting, everyone should have "action plans"—later it was agreed that this would have been too ambitious.

Description of the Vision Meeting Process

Pre-Meeting Data Collection

A four-question survey was distributed to all the parents, teachers and staff of the school (a total of about 90). Approximately 20 of these were returned before the Friday evening meeting. Answers to each question were written up verbatim on flip-chart pages and taped to the walls. All responses were collated by question and written together. Also responses (some quite critical) to a capital campaign survey that had been recently taken up were also put on the wall.

---

*Printed in *Vision in Action: Working with Soul and Spirit in Small Organizations* (Lindisfarne Press, Hudson, NY, 1996), pp. 178–181.
© *1993, Jean W. Yeager, 2245 Miller Road, Chester Springs, PA 19425*

Friday Evening

On Friday evening approximately 50 teachers, parents and friends of the school gathered in the school multipurpose room. As they arrived, many went to the walls to see what was written on the sheets; there they found their own verbatim responses to the questionnaires among the responses of the others.

The purpose of the evening was to introduce the vision weekend agenda and reflect on the history of the school. One teacher who was among the first to join the school recalled moments from the school's past. She recalled a moment when the real "vision" became something definite. An experienced Waldorf teacher had moved from an established school to join their effort. Her dedication to the young children and this school's effort were the inspiration that helped deepen the teacher's commitment and connection with Waldorf education. Her commitment worked as a catalyst that helped the teachers at that time to say, "Yes, we are a Waldorf school" and to move away from the community that had nourished the school to that point.

Following these biographical remarks, the chairperson of the Board recalled the recent past to review the history of the last year. He detailed the situation of the past year, town meetings, restructuring, financial condition, and so forth, and reported where the school stood at that time.

The homework from the evening was for those coming back for the weekend to remember "what inspired them to connect their destiny/ lives with this school."

Saturday

Saturday began in a light, social fashion with singing. Following this, the agenda for the visioning process followed this path:

Lemniscate Step 1 / Review of Accomplishments

In small groups participants listed three or four of the most significant accomplishments the school had made in the recent past. A scribe for each group collected answers, writing them on flip-chart pages without editing. These were reported in plenum.

Coffee Break

Lemniscate Step 2 / S-W-O-T Analysis

In plenum each person expressed their thoughts/feelings regarding the Strengths, Weaknesses, Opportunities and Threats to the school.

Review before Lunch

Lemniscate Step 3 / Eurythmy (Giving and Receiving)

In a large circle, everyone paired off facing one another. Oranges were distributed, one to each person. To a verse or music, these were "given" with the right hand by one person in the pair and "received" with the left hand by the partner.

Lemniscate Step 4 / Imagining Alternative Futures

After reflection, participants were to ask themselves: What recent accomplishments were coming from the future? What was yet to be done? What things needed to be changed? What successes from the past could be built upon? Participants were instructed to order their answers in terms of three Dialogues:

- Dialogue with the Spirit
- Dialogue with Each Other
- Dialogue with the Earth (Resources)

Break was not taken. Individuals were asked to get their own coffee, etc., and then return to work.

Lemniscate Step 5 / Collaboratively Editing the Vision

Following the presentation in plenum of Alternative Futures by the small groups, those groups were dissolved and participants were free to select one of three affinity groups that formed around each of the dialogue areas:

- Dialogue with the Spirit—principles, values, ideals
- Dialogue with Each Other—policies, communications
- Dialogue with the Earth—site, money, facilities

Groups were to collaboratively edit into a single grouping the vision sheets from the six groups who had just reported, without excluding anything.

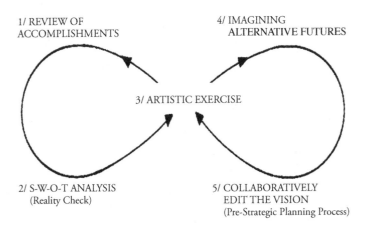

1/ REVIEW OF
ACCOMPLISHMENTS

4/ IMAGINING
ALTERNATIVE FUTURES

3/ ARTISTIC EXERCISE

2/ S-W-O-T ANALYSIS
(Reality Check)

5/ COLLABORATIVELY
EDIT THE VISION
(Pre-Strategic Planning Process)

Closure / Presentation

In plenum, each affinity group presented their edited listings. They appeared to be clear distillations that were harvested from the day's work. Following the presentations there was some time for comment about the process. One sensed that, while there was obviously a great deal still to be done, much had been accomplished during the day.

Comments / Verbatims

Some members expressed amazement that the group went from a "sea" of papers and facts and opinions to a comprehensive, concise vision statement: "How did we wind up with a few, crystal-clear statements from that sea of paper?"

One Board member asked for a reality check: "Are these the vision statements that were really what we want? Is there any disagreement with them?" (Shaking of heads no—no disagreement articulated at that moment.)

Comments from teachers and Board members the following week included:

"We published the vision statement in our weekly Messenger."

"When I read the vision statements, I still get fired up."

"I think this has done most of the work for the strategic planning process."

Endnotes

1. Allan Kaplan, *Development Practitioners and Social Process: Artists of the Invisible* (Pluto Press, London: 1988), pp.115–120.
2. See "Phases of Waldorf School Development," Chapter II of this book.
3. Ibid.
4. Christopher Schaefer and Tÿno Voors, *Vision in Action: Working with Soul and Spirit in Small Organizations* (Lindisfarne Press, Hudson, NY, 1996), pp. 16–23.
5. Source: MIRA: Companions in Development.
6. See Robert Greenleaf, *The Servant as Leader* (Greenleaf Center, Indianapolis, 1981), and Peter Block, *Stewardship: Choosing Service over Self-Interest* (Berrett-Koehler, San Francisco, 1993).
7. See the excellent and provocative study by William Strauss and Neil Howe, *The Fourth Turning: An American Prophecy* (Broadway Books, Random House, NY, 1997), pp. 123–139.
8. See "Phases of Waldorf School Development," Chapter II of this book.
9. Jim Collins, *Good to Great, Why Some Companies Make the Leap...and Others Don't* (HarperCollins, NY, 2001), in particular pp. 90–119. Also *Good to Great and the Social Sectors* (HarperCollins, NY, 2003).
10. Wolfgang Koetker, "How Can Good Waldorf Schools Become Great?" Masters Thesis at Sunbridge College, Spring Valley, NY, 2009.
11. Op. cit., Collins, pp. 174–178.
12. David Cooperrider and Diana Whitney, *Appreciative Inquiry* (Berrett-Koehler, San Francisco, 1999), pp. 1–38.
13. Luigi Morelli, *A Revolution of Hope: Spirituality, Cultural Renewal and Social Change* (Trafford Publishing, Victoria, 2009), pp. 244–268. Also Otto Scharmer, *Theory U: Leading from the Future as It Emerges* (Society for Organizational Learning, Cambridge, MA, 2007), pp. 119–230.
14. Cornelis Pieterse, *Empowerment in Organizations: The Theory and Practice of a Mandate System* (Rudolf Steiner College Press, Fair Oaks, CA, 2006), pp. 99–112. Also Marvin Weisbord, *Discovering Common Ground: How Future Search Conferences Bring People Together to Achieve Breakthrough, Innovation, Empowerment, Shared Vision, and Collaborative Action* (Berrett-Koehler, San Francisco, 1992).
15. Op. cit., Schaefer & Voors, pp. 163–177.
16. Op. cit., Kaplan, pp. 24–29.
17. Peter Drucker, *Managing the Non-Profit Organization: Principles and Practices* (HarperCollins, NY, 1990).
18. A.R.E. Long-Range Plan, 1986.
19. New York Open Center, Mission Statement, draft, 1990.
20. W.K. Kellogg Foundation, *This We Believe*.
21. I am indebted to Professor Mark Kriger of the School of Business, University of New York, for his research on organizational vision.

VII

Rudolf Steiner as Social Thinker and Reformer

*The healing social life is found only when in the mirror of each
human soul the whole community finds its reflection and when in
the community the virtue of each one is living.*

Motto of The Social Ethic
– Rudolf Steiner

In the March 1979 edition of *Kursbuch*, a leftist German
publication, an article appeared with the whimsical title of "Astral Marx:
Rudolf Steiner's Work." The title no doubt refers to the importance that
Steiner placed on the primacy of human consciousness in social change
and societal evolution. In the article the author, Joseph Huber, describes
the work of Rudolf Steiner and of anthroposophy in the following
manner:

> We leftist hares race around madly in pursuit of our socialist
> dreams and when we finally arrive we find an anthroposophical
> hedgehog in place, saying, "Boo! I've been here for ages!" Here
> you find a general hospital, there a cooperative bank; there
> are autonomous kindergartens, schools, publishing houses,
> alternative therapeutic and curative institutions, conference
> centers, free art academies, pharmaceutical firms, biodynamic
> farms and other activities. Whereas the left achieves relatively
> little with much noise, anthroposophists do a lot quietly.[1]

Students of Steiner's work will read such a sentiment with some
amusement while others may ask: Who is Steiner? Wasn't he an
educator, the founder of Waldorf education in the early 20th century?

What does he have to offer us at the beginning of the 21st century? I want to suggest that Steiner's social ideas are profound and relevant to the cultural, political and economic impasse that the modern mindset has produced. Furthermore, the more than eight thousand institutions inspired by his work—ranging from schools, therapeutic centers and communities to banks and companies—offer an extensive body of experience in building up an alternative, cooperative, decentralized and humane society. I am sometimes startled to think of the publicity that Findhorn, the New Age community in Scotland, receives in the Western world and then to reflect on the relative silence with which the work of anthroposophy, with its many communities and initiatives, has been greeted. This introduction to Steiner's social theory and to the practice of working with his ideas is an effort to interest Waldorf parents and a wider public in Steiner as a sociologist, economist and inspirer of new communities, as well as being the founder of Waldorf education.

The Historical and Philosophical Context

Rudolf Steiner was born in 1861 in Lower Austria and died in 1925. After studying natural science and philosophy in Vienna, where he attended the lectures of Franz Brentano at about the same time as did Edmund Husserl (1883), he moved to Weimar to edit the scientific writings of Goethe. While in Weimar, he met many of Germany's leading intellectuals, including Hermann Grimm, Ernst Haeckel and the historian, Heinrich von Treitschke. Here, and later in Berlin, he also read widely in philosophy, history, psychology and sociology and was involved with an astonishing variety of philosophical, spiritual and cultural groups.[2] During this time his spiritual vision was also maturing so that by the early 20th century, Steiner began to give lectures on Spiritual Science and Anthroposophy (Wisdom of the Human Being).

In 1886, while editing Goethe's scientific writings, Steiner published a small book, *A Theory of Knowledge Based on Goethe's World Conception*.[3] This volume provided a philosophical foundation for all of his later work by addressing the relation between the inner world of the human being to the outer world. It also contains some very significant thoughts about the nature of social inquiry. In the section on the spiritual or cultural sciences, he stated that the cultural sciences have as their object of study the human being: "It is human actions, creations, ideas with which we have to do" and that the task or mission of these sciences is to "interpret the human being to himself and to humanity."[4] With these seemingly simple phrases, Rudolf Steiner suggested that the social sciences differ from the natural sciences and that their task is understanding human consciousness as expressed in social creation. Laws, organizational structures, and political, social and economic forms reveal the contours of consciousness; they are external manifestations of the ideas and values of individuals and groups, as was noted in the beginning of this book.

Steiner gave the cultural sciences a dual focus: seeing the individual as the source of social creation and perceiving a pattern in the development of human consciousness through history and the evolution of society. I think it is this dual emphasis on the principle of individuality and on the underlying perspective of history as the drama, the unfolding of humanity toward greater understanding and freedom, that led Steiner to call the social or cultural sciences, the sciences of freedom.

The focus on the individual personality, on the principle of individuality in history also led Steiner to argue that "the particular establishes the general law or principle in the cultural sciences whereas the general establishes the law in the natural sciences."[5] It is the individual event, person, work of art or political manifesto that gives us insight into general patterns—committing Steiner, like Weber, Dilthey and others in the Verstehen tradition of the German cultural sciences, to an ideal-type methodology.

Social Creation and Social Laws

Rudolf Steiner saw a conversation, a meeting between two or more human beings, as the archetypal social phenomenon. Out of such meetings, social creation emerges. It is a simple but not unimportant thought to recognize that nature is not created by us but the social world is. Every conversation, every relationship, every group discussion is a social creation. So are organizations. This is easiest to see when parents are busy starting a new school, or a couple is beginning a new restaurant, or an individual is starting a factory. But existing organizations were once only ideas, and even when they appear successful and massive, they sometimes need to be recreated—as was the recognized need for dramatic changes at IBM in the early 1990s. The same principles apply to the creation and development of nations, or of a united Europe, or of a Russian federation. We continuously create and recreate the fabric of social life. The social world reflects our nature, our ideas and values, while at the same time it shapes consciousness.[6]

Steiner maintained that there were laws in social life as binding as the laws of mechanics. The nature of social laws for Steiner is that they focus on the interplay of human consciousness and social form. In 1898, Steiner formulated what he called the Basic Sociological Law: "At the beginning of culture, humanity strives to create social arrangements in which the interests of the individual are sacrificed for the interest of the whole. Later developments lead to a gradual freeing of the individual from the interests of the community and to an unfolding of individual needs and capacities."[7]

This law or principle exists in time, in all likelihood covering the whole of known history. Certainly, when one ponders the sweep of history and the gradual emergence of individual rights from Greco-Roman times to the present, it appears justified and points to one of the central aspects of historical evolution: the emergence of individual rights and consciousness. Based on my observation of institutional development, I would say that it also applies to the life cycle of institutions; they initially require the energy and sacrifice of the founders in order to be established and then in later years provide more adequately for the needs of their members. Health care and pensions are not priorities in the first few years of an organization's life when survival and growth are the dominant concerns.

In 1905 Steiner described a second principle, calling it the Fundamental Social Law: "The well-being of a community of cooperatively working human beings is the greater the less individuals demand the proceeds of their work for themselves or, in other words, the more they make over these proceeds to their co-workers and the more their needs are met not by their own work but from that of others."[8]

This complex and awkwardly phrased law is concerned with motives, suggesting that when labor is a commodity and self-interest becomes the motive force of economic activity, suffering, poverty, and want are the results. To what degree is the recent global economic crisis or the poverty in the Third World or in our inner cities the result of this social law not being understood in the Western world? What will the long-term social consequences of a modified capitalist system appealing to self-interest really be? Certainly the work of Richard Wilkinson and Kate Pickett in *The Spirit Level: Why Greater Equality Makes Societies Stronger* demonstrates the truth of Steiner's Fundamental Social Law. Those Western societies most committed to market capitalism, the United States and England, have the greatest income inequalities, the highest level of juvenile delinquency, the most domestic violence and the highest prison incarceration rates as well as lower life expectancy than their counterparts in Europe and Asia.[9] High income inequalities produce societies of "somebodies and nobodies" and spread suffering, poverty and want through the world, based on an economic system characterized by market fundamentalism in which we are all encouraged to sell our labor to the highest bidder and to pursue our own self-interests.

There are numerous curative communities, shared-income groups and schools working with Steiner's fundamental social law in a positive manner. The resulting appeal to service, to true motives and to community interest is evident. Do such arrangements produce "well-being"? Steiner not only argued yes, but suggested there would be less mental and physical illness because individuals would make life choices based not on income considerations but on an assessment of their real capacities and interests. Such laws are empirical propositions, accessible to reason and experience and capable of being tested. Although I am not aware of in-depth systematic studies having been conducted on the Fundamental Social Law, the slow but steady progress in human rights, the abolition of slavery, the voting rights of women and equal protection for minority groups in many countries suggests the truth of it. The empirical evidence from public health researchers on the Fundamental Social Law is quite overwhelming, showing that the United States, with the highest income inequalities in the Western world, is headed for social and economic decline with levels of inequality not seen since the Great Depression.

Reflection on such principles suggests that there are, in all likelihood, hundreds of such propositions operative in social life. For example, the larger and the newer the group, the more structured the leadership required to have an effective group process; or its reverse, the smaller and older the group, the less structured leadership is required. Another example is that the more an institution is willing to learn from its history and experience—the more it delights in being a learning community—the more successful it will be in coping with the future. Such principles, even when quite mundane, can make an appeal to our consciousness and thereby help to create a healthier society.

The Evolution of Human Consciousness

Steiner regarded it as important to understand how the social world reflects human consciousness. He was radical in many of his political and social ideas, suggesting that modern economic and political forms do little to challenge the individual to develop, but instead enhance forces of egotism and passivity. To explore these ideas and, indeed, to grasp the basis of his social thought, requires some acquaintance with his historical perspective. This I can do only in the briefest manner.

Steiner saw human evolution moving from a oneness with nature and the divine world, a form of consciousness which Owen Barfield calls "original participation" in prehistory, to increasing separation from both nature and the spiritual world.[10] The march of civilizations from China, India and Persia through Egypt, Greece and Rome to modern civilization is for him the story of the gradual unfolding of individual human consciousness and of the growing awareness and exploration of the physical sense world. Ancient cultures were hierarchical and theocratic in nature, with royalty and priests or priestesses acting as both guides for society and mediators with the divine world. Spiritual beings, the gods, were experienced by large numbers of people as eminently real, more real than the world of the senses, the world of *maya*. With Greek and Roman culture, political and state forms were developed in which the question of citizenship, of rights and responsibilities, arose and in which art and literature revealed a marked interest in the physical sense world, in the human form and in the human personality. The spiritual world was now only experienced through ceremony, myth and legend. With the Renaissance, Steiner saw a further development, a further individualization process in consciousness and a deepening incarnation into the physical world. Modern science and technology developed and a more conscious economic system came into being, culminating in the world economy of the present. The dominant social forms moved from theocracies, committed to religious and cultural life, to political and legal rights in Greek and Roman times and the industrial and post-industrial order of the present. This evolution is the external manifestation of an internal change in which, gradually, the sense-oriented individual consciousness of the modern human being emerges.[11]

Such an evolutionary process of consciousness has a number of consequences. It enhances the possibility of human freedom, but it also unleashes increased antisocial forces in the individual and in society. As we become more aware of self, of what we think, feel, and want as individuals, we lose our "social instincts, our natural understanding of others." Steiner felt that in our time and in the coming centuries, all social instincts will be lost and we will increasingly be "hermits wandering through the world." This natural evolutionary tendency brings with it the possibility of self-knowledge and self-development, but it has the social consequence of separating individuals and groups so that we become strangers to one another. The forces of critical intelligence, doubt, likes and dislikes and egotism in our intentional life turn us increasingly into antisocial beings, desperately longing for love and understanding but incapable of offering it to others.[12]

Steiner saw the development of modern consciousness leading toward increasing fragmentation and violence unless it is met by a variety of countermeasures. He described three antidotes in particular. The first was the need to develop a conscious new social understanding, a practical social science that would generate a new interest in others and in social life. He gave a thorough understanding of the four temperaments and of the stages of human development as examples for a new form of social understanding suggesting that such knowledge would open our eyes to the uniqueness of the other. I see many efforts in modern psychology and sociology as efforts to respond to this need, to supplement more traditional understandings of communication, relationships, group work, family life and society with more contemporary approaches appealing to consciousness and individual responsibility.

A second countermeasure, and one which is critical for an understanding of his social theory and for Waldorf education, is the need to develop new social forms that make visible our interdependency as human beings and that encourage us to meet and work together at deeper levels. Partnership forms and collegial relationships based on equality may not always be efficient, but they encourage us to meet, allowing our mutual destiny, our karma, to unfold. Indeed, this latter point was of critical concern to Steiner. He believed that the loss of social instincts in modern society would result in the loss of social creativity because true human meetings would become ever more difficult. All hierarchical social forms, by dividing people into levels and highly specialized roles, would only enhance the antisocial nature of the age. He felt that not only new organizational forms were needed to cope with this antisocial trend, but that a totally new societal structure was called for, which he called the Threefold Social Order and which he publicly presented to different audiences in Europe from 1917–1922 as a way out of the chaos of World War I.

Steiner saw a third antidote to the antisocial nature of modern Western consciousness in a conscious process of individual inner development, of inner transformation and spiritual awakening. He described the essential nature of such a transformation in numerous lectures and in his book, *Knowledge of Higher Worlds and Its Attainment*.[13] Such a process involves utilizing individual consciousness to order and transform our soul capacities of thinking, feeling and willing, so that doubt is transformed into interest, likes and dislikes into empathetic understanding and egotism into acts of compassion. This inner transformation further requires a process of moral and spiritual development, of pursuing a conscious meditative path.

Steiner's sociological and historical orientation leads to four basic insights that are woven into the fabric of this book. The first is that a more equitable, just and humane society requires both societal change and spiritual transformation. Societal change and individual development are the twin pillars of our social future. This was recognized by many in the late 1960s and early 1970s. It is also clearly expressed in Steiner's Motto of The Social Ethic, quoted at the beginning of this essay.

A second insight is the recognition that we are all social artists and social scientists. The medium, the color of this art is our own nature—the combination of soul and spirit qualities we bring into a conversation, a relationship, an office. The main requirement of the social art, as with all arts, is that we are aware and willing to enter openly into the demands of the moment. Having gotten involved in a dispute with a colleague or having reviewed the budget, we can reflect and discover underlying principles: that group development requires clear goals and a deepening level of trust, or that conflict mechanisms mainly lie in the realm of perceptions, or that budgets reflect our actual values and priorities. So, in daily life, we move between moments of social art and social science and by bringing them to consciousness, we become more conscious co-creators of our social world, as described in Chapter I.

Third, Steiner pointed to the need to create new, non-hierarchical organizational and societal forms that encourage human development and combat the natural egotism of our age. This is the central thought underlying the non-hierarchical collegial forms of Waldorf schools and other communities inspired by his work.[14]

The fourth basic perspective which Steiner brought to the question of social reform, is the recognition that all societies have a threefold nature and that cultural, political and economic life now need to be organized according to different principles so that the heavy hand of the state or the unwarranted domination of capital can be avoided.

The Threefold Social Order and the Practice of Social Renewal

The year 1917 can be seen as a turning point in modern history. It was the year of the Russian Revolution, in which Lenin and the Bolsheviks came to power, and it was also the year in which the United States overcame its isolationist tendencies and entered World War I. Europe was engaged in a world war which brought about its decline and marked the end of the nineteenth century social and political order. Out of this war experience, Rudolf Steiner gave birth to a threefold imagination of the human being and tried to show how this imagination could lead to healing social forms. Although the outlines of the threefold social order were already contained in his two communications to the German and Austrian governments in July, it was in November of 1917 that these ideas were first publicly presented in a series of lectures called "Anthroposophy and the Academic Sciences," later to be published in 1919 as *Toward Social Renewal*.[15]

The threefold image of the human being relates the psychological faculties of thinking, feeling and willing to the physiological functions of the nerve-sense system, the working of heart and lung, and the metabolic limb system, which includes the digestive system and arms and legs. In the same way that the three physiological systems of the human being are semi-independent, yet serve the totality of the human organism, so too, according to Steiner, should the three realms of cultural, political and economic life, while serving the whole of society, have a certain independence. For Rudolf Steiner, the dominant value of cultural life is freedom; that of political-legal life, equality; and that of economic life, cooperation and fraternity. This implies a structural principle separating cultural life from that of the state and also creating a separate administrative form for economic life based on associations of producers, consumers and traders/retailers.

Upon first coming into contact with the ideas of the Threefold Social Order, one can easily think, "Oh, another abstract utopian model." Yet, if we seriously reflect on the nature of cultural activities such as teaching, artistic activity or research, we realize that the essential character of such cultural activity is based upon the free initiative of the individual. Ultimately, it is the creativity of the individual that matters in law, education, medicine, architecture and the arts. Steiner is, therefore, describing a reality when he maintains that the cultural realm should be organized to enhance the freedom and creativity of the individual. Choice in education, through a variety of self-administered schools in which teachers and parents work together to provide the best education possible, should be the model. This would mean an educational system in which many different types of schools and colleges, all free of state control—such as Montessori and Waldorf schools but also Buddhist academies, Science and Art high schools, and Catholic and Christian academies—would all be competing for the interest and loyalty of students and parents. It is competition which Steiner saw as positive for education and cultural life, not the bureaucratic straitjacket of state or public education, which out of political necessity works toward a standardized curriculum.

Steiner saw the main purpose of the state as the formulation and administration of law, of legal norms. He did not envision state involvement in education or in economic life because this would produce distortions and inefficiencies. In the area of rights, it is the principle of equality, exercised in a democratic process, which is critical. If the state is significantly involved in other activities, then special interest groups and, in particular, powerful corporations are tempted to distort the process of decision making, a danger that Steiner foresaw in many societies, including the United States.

Steiner developed fundamentally new ideas in economics and published them in a series of lectures in 1922 as *World Economy*.[16] For him the basic activity of economic life is providing the goods and services needed by people. Steiner saw the invisible hand doctrine and the concept of enlightened self-interest as formulated by Adam Smith in his *Wealth of Nations* as a mental straitjacket that distorted the meaning of work and of economic processes. We work for meaning, not mainly for profit. The motive power of economic production is essentially to serve human needs as efficiently as possible. For Steiner, economic activity, at its heart, is a cooperative, communal activity, not a competitive struggle for profit and survival, as conventional economics would have it. If we follow this line of thinking, then economic life, including the allocation of resources and the settling of price levels, would be the result of cooperative decisions between producer, consumer, and retail organizations at local and regional levels. As Steiner put it, "Not laws but men, using their immediate insights and interests, would regulate the circulation and consumption of goods."[17] Steiner's ideas in economics contain other, quite radical notions. He favored removing land from speculation and private ownership and saw leasing arrangements (i.e., land trusts) as important. He also argued that company ownership should not be private as such and passed on to succeeding generations of the owning families but should be made available to the best management talent in each generation. Like many recent economists and social thinkers such as David Korten and Kevin Philips, he was intensely concerned about the manipulation of economic activity by financial and capital institutions, seeing that this would subordinate human needs at local, national, and international levels to speculative financial interests.[18]

One of Steiner's central concerns regarding economic activity was, as was Karl Marx's, the commodity character of labor. He repeatedly insisted that wage questions and other issues connected to the conditions of work be separated from economic processes and be regulated by rights groups, according to the needs of individuals and the prevailing sense of equity. This idea was already referred to in the presentation of Steiner's fundamental social law. Steiner's approach to wages is so at variance with prevailing opinion in Western capitalistic societies that we fail to see the ways in which the tax system and the bargaining process between management and labor already reflect something of his view, although in a distorted manner.[19]

Steiner as Social Reformer and Activist

The threefold image of the human being and of society provided the foundation upon which Rudolf Steiner and his co-workers sought to influence the restructuring of European society and the peace negotiations in Versailles in 1917. These efforts not only involved many lectures, multiple conversations with individuals, private letters to people of political influence and a public appeal to the German nation, but also led to an attempt to send copies of General von Moltke's private diaries to the Versailles Peace Conference in order to show the inaccuracy and one-sidedness of the "war guilt clause."[20]

While the attempts to help end the war in 1917 and to influence the peace negotiations in Versailles failed, Rudolf Steiner proceeded to elaborate his ideas for a new social structure in his book *Toward Social Renewal* (1919), which received wide distribution. He also founded the League for the Threefold Social Order in Germany and Switzerland in order to carry these ideas into practical life. A weekly paper, *The Threefold Social Order*, was started, for which he wrote many of the lead articles, and he gave many lectures on a variety of social and political themes throughout Germany and Switzerland. Some of these lectures and articles are available in English in *The Renewal of the Social Organism* and *Spiritual Science as a Foundation for Social Forms*.[21]

As part of the activity of the League for the Threefold Social Order, Rudolf Steiner and co-workers such as Carl Unger, Emil Molt, Emil Leinhas, Ernst Uehli and Hans Kuhn met in late 1919 to discuss the possibilities of creating a variety of working associative forms such as a bank or a stock company. The first Waldorf school in Stuttgart had already grown out of the activity of Rudolf Steiner and the League, and it was hoped that other successful models would follow. So on New Year's evening 1919 it was decided to create "The Coming Day—A Stock Company to Further Economic and Spiritual Values." In time it was to embrace some twenty organizations, including farms, the Waldorf school, research institutes, chemical factories, two printing companies, and the Waldorf Astoria Cigarette Factory. This practical experiment in the application of threefold ideas is not well known in the English-speaking world, yet it is worth studying despite its eventual closing in 1924 because of hyper-inflation in Germany.[22]

In late 1922, attacked by a rising tide of nationalistic and fascist elements, Rudolf Steiner withdrew from his extensive public efforts to influence social, economic and political events. He remarked, "I knew that people had not yet achieved sufficient maturity and insight, yet the attempt had to be made, for I might well have been wrong." His social ideas were radical, egalitarian and anti-nationalistic. The people of Central Europe were not ready to receive them.[23]

Steiner and the Social Future

In what way are Steiner's social and economic ideas relevant today and how can we judge their efficacy? If we reflect on the combination of the global environmental, social and economic crises of the present, we can agree with the preamble of the United Nations Earth Charter:

We stand at a critical moment in Earth's history, a time when humanity must choose its future. As the world becomes increasingly interdependent and fragile, the future at once holds great peril and great promise. …We must join together to bring forth a sustainable global society founded on respect for nature, universal human rights, economic justice and a culture of peace.[24]

For Steiner such a choice required a multifaceted spiritual awakening, a new and more balanced view of science and knowledge and a new formative threefold imagination of society. While he was active in a very different time, almost one hundred years ago, he felt that a new, more spiritual consciousness was already beginning and would grow stronger in the coming centuries. Such an awakening would also lead to new forms of psychological and spiritual knowledge and to new societal forms. Furthermore, he saw the deeply rooted desire for freedom, equality and fraternity (brotherhood and sisterhood) as an unconscious force in human hearts which would gradually lead to a threefold membering of society.

Looking at developments in the last fifty years, we can discern the following transformational shifts which create new opportunities for fundamental social reform:

- A multifaceted and widespread spiritual awakening which is leading millions of people to see themselves, the spiritual and divine world, and the earth differently. All spiritual traditions and practices from past and present cultures are now available in books and on the internet, and study groups, meditation groups, self-help groups and social action groups abound in many parts of the world. As Peter Drucker, the well known management expert, stated some years ago:

  > Every few hundred years in Western history there occurs a sharp transformation. Within a few short decades, society —its world view, its basic values, its social and political structures, its arts, its key institutions—rearranges itself. And the people born then cannot even imagine a world in which their grandparents lived and into which their own parents were born. We are currently living through such a transformation.[25]

- As part of this transformation, a new, more holistic view of science and knowledge is emerging which questions the one-sidedness of Western reductionist materialistic science and technology. Willis Harmon, the visionary thinker, futurist and author of *Global Mind Change* noted:

This emerging trans-modern world view, involves a shift in the locus of authority from external to "inner knowing." It has basically turned away from the older scientific view... and trusts perceptions of the wholeness and spiritual aspects of organisms, ecosystems, Gaia and Cosmos. This implies a spiritual reality and ultimate trust in the authority of the whole. It amounts to a reconciliation of scientific inquiry with the "perennial wisdom" at the core of the world's spiritual traditions.[26]

- The emergence of a distinct new global values sub-culture which Paul Ray and associates call the "Cultural Creatives," who combine an open spirituality, concerns about social equity, cultural diversity and environmental responsibility. According to Ray and Anderson, this group constitutes about twenty-six percent of the adult population in the United States and similar percentages in Europe and parts of Asia.[27] The "Cultural Creatives" are in the vanguard of the "sharp transformation" described by Drucker and constitute the great majority of parents in Waldorf schools. They are estimated to number 200 million people worldwide.

- They also constitute the bulk of the "civil society" movement, which came to public awareness through the "battle in Seattle" by opposing the excesses of globalization, and which consists of millions of groups of all races and classes who are not waiting for economic or political elites to right the wrongs of the world but are acting to reconstitute this world. The importance of this underground movement, which Paul Hawken movingly describes in *Blessed Unrest*, lies in its ability to bring to consciousness the full range of environmental and human concerns and to insist that an unholy and manipulative alliance between "big business" and "big government" is no longer acceptable.[28] So we now have the beginnings of a free cultural life, a diffuse international civil society movement as a third locus of power which can ask meaningful questions about the appropriate roles of economic life, of government and of cultural and spiritual life, as well as being busy creating a new and emerging future.

These developments have been given a further jolt by the recent global economic crisis as it, like Hurricane Katrina and New Orleans, reveals the corruption of political and economic elites and calls into question the viability of market capitalism. With the fall of Communism in 1989 and the crisis of capitalism in 2007–2008, the two dominant political and economic systems of the post-World War II period have been called into question. There is now space to consider a new imagination of society, such as that offered by Steiner from 1917–1922, for it is clear that a multifaceted search is now underway for alternatives to the present social, economic and political impasse.

While fundamental changes in outlook and values are occurring globally, the large established institutions of society will not lead the change to a new, freer, more equitable and sustainable society, for they have too much at stake in supporting the status quo. They will allow tinkering at the margins but not a fundamental reordering of priorities and a basic redesign of political, social and economic systems. Such work will need to be done by the "Blessed Unrest," by the great number of local, regional, national and international civil society groups, using a tri-sectoral approach of calling together people from business, government and civil society to address issues of public concern. Out of a new, more holistic and spiritual consciousness and with a new set of values and experiences, much can continue to be accomplished. It will often seem like "crossing the river by feeling for stones," a phrase coined by Chen Yun, a compatriot of Deng Xiaoping, who together master-minded China's reforms and development after 1978. It will require creating new institutions and new practices, new facts on the ground, strong enough to withstand the uncertainties and crises of the current political and economic order. In this emerging practice the principles of threefolding, of liberty, equality and fraternity, can be a guiding imagination and the experience of the thousands of institutions inspired by Rudolf Steiner's work, a source of strength, as well as a partner in mutual learning and development.[29]

Building New Communities:
Practical Applications of Steiner's Social Ideas

Anthroposophy as a worldwide spiritual movement has about fifty thousand members, yet it is estimated that it supports and is connected to a decentralized institutional network of between eight thousand to ten thousand groups and institutions and touches the lives of millions of people. The best known of these is the Waldorf School Movement, with about two hundred schools in North America, and over a thousand worldwide. Connected to the school movement are adult education and training centers such as Rudolf Steiner College in Sacramento; the Center for Anthroposophy in Wilton, New Hampshire; the Sunbridge Institute in Spring Valley, New York; and the Rudolf Steiner Institute and the Waldorf Institute of Southern California. There are five larger adult education and teacher training centers in North America and fifty or so worldwide, with full- or part-time enrollment of some eight thousand students. Included in this number are numerous art and eurythmy schools, therapy training institutes and other specialized adult educational institutions, as well as some universities such as Alanus and Witten-Herdecke in Germany and Rudolf Steiner University College in Oslo.

A second field of institutional work is biodynamic agriculture and farming, with many farms and gardens in Europe and a growing number in the United States and other parts of the world. Many of the developing community-supported agriculture (CSA) projects have a close link with biodynamic agriculture and with Steiner's work. One of the central concerns of the biodynamic movement is the healing of the earth through developing a whole or a diversified farm organism and removing farmland from private ownership through land trusts and other forms of common ownership.

Significant work on social questions has also been done in the many communities dedicated to working with people in need of special care, in particular the Camphill communities. These residential villages integrate staff and villagers into houses, viewing everyone as an integral part of village life. Houses have budgets and families have a living allowance but no salaries. Indeed, Steiner's fundamental social law is worked with intensively in these villages, as are the principles of the Threefold Social Order.

An international association of organization development consultants with a special connection to Steiner's work has developed called the Association for Social Development (ASD). This group of about one hundred twenty consultants has been built up around the pioneering work of the Dutch psychiatrist Bernard Lievegoed and the Netherlands Pedagogical Institute (NPI). Here, too, the social and economic ideas of Steiner play a central role, both in how these groups are organized and in the methodology and content of their work.

A growing number of banks and financial institutions also acknowledge a special debt to Steiner and seek to work with money in new ways. This involves asking depositors to choose the project, size and interest rate of their investments and encouraging an understanding of and a working with the different qualities of loan money, gift money and purchase money. A prime example of this successful work is the Triodos Bank in Holland, the largest "Green Bank" in Europe today. In the United States the Rudolf Steiner Foundation in San Francisco brings a new awareness into the social financing of its many new projects as well as into its philanthropic work.

The number of shops, retail organizations and companies that, in one way or another, are linked to the work of anthroposophy is legion. For instance, Naturata, a health food chain in Germany, and Weleda, the manufacturer of medicine and body care products, and countless other commercial organizations work with ideas drawn from Steiner's work. Sometimes this finds expression in searching for new forms of ownership, or in a producer association of companies that help each other in financing expansion, or in still other organizations that work in new ways with leadership questions and wages. The list of institutions connected to anthroposophy can be extended to include institutions for the care of the elderly, such as the Fellowship Community in Spring Valley, New York, environmental and research centers, artistic, building, and architectural cooperatives, as well as many other kinds of initiatives.

The healing arts and medicine is another area where work is done with some larger hospitals, many therapy centers and clinics, as well as with medical associations active in the training and education of doctors and nurses. Underlying this work is a different view of illness and modes of treatment that rely on homeopathic principles of healing. As many of the clinics have patient associations, different social principles are also worked with. This work is most developed in Holland, Germany and Brazil, with over five hundred medical doctors practicing anthroposophically-extended medicine in Holland and hospitals such as the Filder Clinic and the teaching Hospital at Witten-Herdecke in Germany practicing anthroposophically-oriented medicine.

What is common to most of these institutions is that they are of small to medium size, quite decentralized in structure, often committed to non-hierarchical values and to practicing ecologically sound principles. Decision making by consensus is worked with in many of these organizations, particularly those in education and cultural life. Money and wages are often dealt with in quite unconventional ways, and spiritual values and questions are openly discussed.

This presentation of institutional activity inspired by Steiner's work does not constitute an analysis or evaluation. However the longevity of these institutional networks and their multi-sectoral experiences, when coupled with their socially innovative practices, do contain many lessons, which, together with the experiences and insights of thousands of other alternative institutions, offer the best hope for building a new society. They do suggest a lesson critical to our social future: A new, more spiritual conception of the world and of the human being leads to the creation of a more equal, just and sustainable economic and social reality which, in turn, works to foster a more widespread holistic consciousness.

We are at a turning point in Western society where, individually and collectively, choices need to be made if a society characterized by environmental degradation, great inequality and selfishness and fear is not to undermine the essentially human. In this process of choice, Waldorf school communities and other institutions inspired by Rudolf Steiner's work can engage in dialog and research with the many other groups and individuals also on a path of inner and outer transformation. Those not familiar with the scope of Steiner's work or with Waldorf education need to put aside their distaste of philosophical complexity and examine the body of experience evident in the many communities inspired by his innovative social ideas, while the Waldorf world could more openly explore the many meaningful spiritual, psychological and social insights developed by other groups and movements also interested in a healthier social future.

Endnotes

1. Joseph Huber and Astral Marx, Rudi Lissau, trans., *The Work of Rudolf Steiner and Anthroposophy* (Kursbuch, Frankfurt, March 1979), p. 77.
2. Rudolf Steiner, *Autobiography: The Course of My Life* (Anthroposphic Press, Hudson, NY, 1999), pp. 111–120.
3. Rudolf Steiner, *A Theory of Knowledge Based on Goethe's World Conception* (Anthroposophic Press, Hudson, NY, 1968), p. 101.
4. Ibid., p. 102.
5. Ibid., p. 103.
6. See Chapter I for an elaboration of these points.
7. Translated by the author from *Geiteswissenschaft und Soziale Frage*, Dornach, GA 34, p. 56.
8. Rudolf Steiner, *Anthroposophy and the Social Question* (Anthroposphic Press, Spring Valley, NY, 1987), p. 32.
9. Richard Wilkinson and Kate Pickett, *The Spirit Level: Why Equality Makes Societies Stronger* (Bloomsbury Press, New York, 2009). See pp. 49–173 for a full presentation of the research.
10. Owen Barfield, *Saving the Appearances: A Study of Idolatry* (Wesleyan University Press, Middletown, CT, 1977).
11. See Stewart Easton for a comprehensive overview of Steiner's view on historical evolution, *Rudolf Steiner: Herald of a New Epoch* (Anthroposophic Press, Spring Valley, NY, 1980).
12. Rudolf Steiner, *Social and Anti-Social Forces* (Mercury Press, Spring Valley, NY, 1992).
13. Rudolf Steiner, *How to Know Higher Worlds* (Anthroposophic Press, Hudson, NY, 1994).
14. Op. cit., Steiner, *Social and Anti-Social Forces*.
15. Rudolf Steiner, *Toward Social Renewal* (Rudolf Steiner Press, London, 1977).
16. Rudolf Steiner, *World Economy: The Foundation of a Science of World Economics* (Rudolf Steiner Press, London, 1949).
17. Op. cit., Steiner, *World Economy*, p. 107.
18. David Korten, *Agenda for a New Economy* (Berrett-Koehler Publishers, San Francisco, 2009).
19. Rudolf Steiner, *Anthroposophy and the Social Question* (Anthroposophic Press, Spring Valley, NY, 1987).
20. For a detailed description of Steiner's social, political and economic initiatives from 1917–1922, see Hans Kuhn, *Dreigliederungs-Zeit: Rudolf Steiner's Kampf für die Gesellschaft* (Philosophisch-Anthroposophisher Verlag, Dornach, 1978).

21. Both available from SteinerBooks, Great Barrington, MA.
22. Op. cit., Kuhn.
23. Ibid.
24. United Nations Earth Charter, Preamble. Passed in 2000, it contains sixteen principles for a sustainable future.
25. Peter Drucker, *Post-Capitalist Society* (Harper, New York, 1993), p. 18.
26. Willis Harmon, quote and interview about *Global Mind Change* (Knowledge Systems, Indianapolis, 1988), available through Wikipedia.
27. Paul Ray and Sherry Anderson, *The Cultural Creatives* (Three River Press, New York, 2000), pp. 7–42.
28. Paul Hawken, *Blessed Unrest* (Viking, New York, 2007).
29. For an excellent study and description of threefold and tri-sectoral approaches to social reform see Martin Large, *Common Wealth: For a Free, Equal, Mutual and Sustainable Society* (Hawthorn Press, Stroud, UK, 2009).

This essay first appeared in ReVision, *Fall 1992, and has been modified for inclusion in this book.*

VIII

The Experience of Hope: Waldorf Schools as Cathedrals of the 21st Century

'Tis curious that we only believe as deep as we live.
– Emerson

I believe that Waldorf schools are seeds for a new society, not only because of their curriculum and because they educate children to be healthy, creative adults, but because in their activities and practices they embody a deep inner wisdom, a new world view which celebrates the human being as a responsible steward of the earth and member of a life-affirming society. In this essay I seek to elaborate this wisdom described as mysteries or sacraments and in so doing use the metaphor of the European cathedral, not because it is a Christian church, but because it represents a school, an ark, for a new age in the development of Western culture.

The Medieval World and the Gothic Cathedral

The century and a half between 1130 and 1280 witnessed the high point of medieval civilization. It was the golden age of the troubadours, and it was the time in which *Parzival* and *Lohengrin* were written. Albertus Magnus, Thomas Aquinas, St. Elizabeth and St. Francis were all alive and renewing the Church with new knowledge and a new piety. The great monastic orders, the Cistercians and Dominicans, were fostering a revival of agriculture, the healing arts and scholarship. The Knights Templar provided safety for travelers and laid the foundation for our modern economic system.

It is hard for us to enter the medieval mind, to experience the drama of salvation as the central focus of medieval life. As one historian notes: "The workings of God, or the devil, or the Virgin Mary, the states of sin and salvation, the expectation of the kingdom of Heaven, these were living principles that effectively underlay and motivated the Christian's world."[1]

During the High Middle Ages, a remarkable community-building impulse unfolded: the building of the cathedrals. Over two hundred cathedrals and many more churches, abbeys and monasteries were built between 1130 and 1280. They were mainly Gothic in France and Romanesque and later Gothic in Germany. The cathedrals in Chartres, Paris, Amiens, Soissons, at Lincoln, Canterbury, Salisbury and Wells, in Cologne, Bonn, and Ulm and in Bruges and Antwerp all stem from this period. The medieval cathedral- and church-building activity involved generations of craftsmen and absorbed over one-third of what we now call the gross national product (GNP). We have no adequate explanation for such an amazing outpouring of creativity. In his work on the rose windows, Painton Cowen remarks, "We can see only that something prompted people of all trades and classes to undertake a venture that resulted in workmanship and inspiration of a degree rarely equaled in the history of mankind and acted to weld together communities and to embrace generations."[2] In *Civilization*, Kenneth Clark describes the building of Chartres:

> Men and women came from far away carrying heavy burdens of provisions for the workmen, ...wine, oil, corn. Amongst them were lords and ladies, pulling carts with the rest. There was perfect discipline and a most profound silence. All hearts were united and each man forgave his enemies.[3]

The Gothic cathedral was built out of the ogive, the vaulted arch. Its form works on the human being, stressing uprightness and verticality, enhancing the experience of individuality.

In *Art and Human Consciousness*, Gottfried Richter describes the Gothic cathedral in the following manner: "The upward-striving force in its columns grows and grows until it eats its way into the heavy beams, shatters their horizontality and turns them upright to form pointed arches."[4] The walls, in turn, are broken up with luminous stained glass windows depicting the saints and the work of the Redeemer. They are windows into the beyond, into the spirit.

The cathedrals were many things to the communities in which they existed and to the pilgrims who came form afar to visit the holy shrines. They were, first of all, schools of adult education, or folk schools for the lay person, the common man. Through ritual, picture, sculpture and form, they portrayed the drama of salvation and the redeeming power of Christ and the saints.[5] Secondly, they were places of community celebration through the many feast days and the celebration of the seven sacraments, culminating in the sacrament of life, Holy Communion. They were also places of private inspiration where individuals, both lay and clergy, nobility and beggar, could come to commune with themselves and their God. Most importantly, the cathedral was a vessel, an ark, for forming human consciousness in a transition time in human history, a time poised between the glories of the ancient world and the new world of science, rationality and individual consciousness. Their form and content worked powerfully upon individuals to bring about a new awareness of the human individuality as a responsible and divinely endowed being.

Building these vessels for the spirit involved an extensive community partnership between the various estates of medieval society. The clergy not only carried the sacraments of the church, functioning as intermediaries between the human and spiritual worlds; they also provided inspiration and the design for the cathedral, as well as fostering the development of the craft schools and guilds so that builders, masons, stonecutters and artisans had the skills to carry out a work of enormous scale and complexity. The craft guilds themselves functioned as training schools and communities of support, drawing on generations of families to provide particular skills for the building enterprise. The Christian lay orders, and in particular the Knights Templar, collected funds and gave extensively of their own endowment to further the building of cathedrals throughout Europe. The nobility gave financial and state support, while people of all classes in the towns and countryside gave of their time and their provisions to make the building possible. Moved by a mighty community spirit, these groups came together to build masterpieces of beauty in the centers of towns and cities, rivaling in grandeur the temples of ancient times.

A Time of Transition

The cathedrals were built in a time of historical transition. We are again at such a time 850 years later. The individualized scientific and technical mindset of Western culture has reached a limit despite the seemingly massive power of corporations, governments and large universities. Concern about the environment, about health, education and social justice grows, and with it comes a questioning of the materialistic values underlying our consumer societies. Starting in the early part of the 20th century and spurred by the horrors of two world wars, a multifaceted psychological and spiritual awakening is occurring among individuals and groups throughout the Western world. Over one-half of U.S. adults report having religious or spiritual experiences, and over ten percent are on a systematic path of inner development using prayer and meditation.[6] Growing numbers of people see the Earth as a living being and experience the necessity for humanity to consciously connect to the divine.

Rudolf Steiner suggested that 1899 marked the end of the Dark Age (Kali Yuga), a 5000-year period in which humanity needed to gradually lose its direct connection to spiritual realities in order to develop greater individual consciousness and freedom. He pointed to the 20th century as the beginning of a new age in which spiritual experiences and the development of a new spiritual wisdom were possible. He used his own clairvoyance and his education in science and philosophy to elaborate a spiritual science, insisting that the principles of natural science needed to be extended to include the investigation of spiritual realities. It was out of this research that in 1917–1918 he presented a comprehensive picture of the human being as a threefold being of body, soul and spirit. This investigation of the human being as the bridge between spirit and matter, and his detailed research into the physiological, psychological and spiritual basis of human development became the basis for Waldorf education in 1919.

Presently, this school movement of over 1000 schools, 1400 kindergartens and many teacher education institutes exists on all established continents and works within all major religious and ethnic groups. The Waldorf school curriculum is also being increasingly adapted to the needs of public education in the United States, with charter schools, magnet schools and pilot projects in New York, Milwaukee, Sacramento, San Diego, Detroit and other cities.

Waldorf School Communities as Cathedrals of the 21st Century

Why choose the image of the cathedral to describe the cultural task of Waldorf education in this time? The answer lies in the pivotal role that the cathedrals played in the transitional time of the High Middle Ages. As previously noted, they expressed the central focus of medieval life, the longing for salvation and at the same time were vessels for building community and fostering a new individual consciousness. Waldorf school communities can serve a similar cultural role in this time of transition to a new, more ecological and socially aware spiritual consciousness. To do so, however, the Waldorf movement will need to bring to greater consciousness and articulation the social and spiritual wisdom it embodies. This articulation, this deciphering entails bringing to awareness the spiritual and social mysteries embedded in the education, much like reading the meanings of the wonderful iconography of the Gothic cathedrals in which every statue, window, door and column had its particular significance. The thoughts that follow are a beginning, a still-tentative effort to begin such a sounding in the hope that other voices will add their distinctive notes and that we may together uncover the broader tasks of Waldorf education for the 21st century.

The Physical, Social and Pedagogical Architecture of Waldorf Schools

The medieval cathedrals have a marvelous physical architecture that supported community life and made manifest in color, form and ritual the form and structure of the medieval world view. Waldorf schools, when purpose-built, also have a unique way of working with color and form and adapting to the cultural and natural landscape of their surroundings. Waldorf school buildings in Hungary, Germany, Wales, India, Brazil and Canada work with different materials and styles, yet they are all efforts to provide worthy, light-filled spaces for nurturing the soul and spirit of children.[7] For many people, entering a Waldorf kindergarten for the first time is an awe-inspiring, affirmative experience. The beauty of the room, the colored scarves, natural objects, small tables and chairs and poetic pictures invite us into the heart of early childhood. A part of us longs to enter this magic kingdom again, to play, listen to fairy tales and bake bread. But also the other classrooms and the halls and meeting spaces in purpose-built Waldorf schools can inspire us and lead us to wish that we had gone to school here.

The physical architecture supports a social architecture: the community of a teacher and a class of students, the partnership between teachers, parents and administrators for the sake of the children's development. Usually being independent of state control, Waldorf schools are also institutions of the free spiritual life, not needing to satisfy the many educational and bureaucratic requirements of county or state.

Given the unique relationship between the class teacher, the children and the class parents, and the formally non-hierarchical, collegial nature of decision making between the teachers and Board, we can experience the intentional, destiny-forming quality of Waldorf school forms. The Gothic cathedrals were communities in which the priesthood, the artisans and craftsmen, the nobility and the local citizens came together to celebrate the mystery of salvation. Waldorf schools are destiny communities in which the teachers, parents, children, administrators and friends come together to celebrate the mysteries of human incarnation and of child development.

In addition to the social architecture of Waldorf schools, there is a pedagogical architecture manifest in the detailed, developmentally-appropriate and richly artistic curriculum. This curriculum is based on a specific picture of child development, the gradual unfolding of the physical, psychological and cognitive capacities of children. These pedagogical insights are succinctly captured in the phrase "education from the inside out," as printed on popular Waldorf bumper stickers. Extensive resource materials are available in English and many other languages, both on the Waldorf curriculum and the underlying view of child development.[8]

Within the physical, social and pedagogical forms of Waldorf school communities, the mysteries of the human being as a being of body, soul and spirit are celebrated. It is no longer, as in the Middle Ages, a celebration of the drama of salvation that is being enacted, but rather a celebration of the free human being who is capable of becoming a responsible co-creator with the gods. This celebration takes place through a largely implicit recognition of and practice with what I call the seven mysteries of Waldorf education, which I will attempt to describe.

The Mysteries of the Free Human Being in Waldorf Education

In reflecting on the mysteries that are enacted daily in Waldorf schools, I wish to draw attention to seven sacramental activities or processes that together constitute the "Art of Education." The first of these is the mystery of human incarnation and of human development fostered through a proper education. This mystery involves helping the individual child as a being of soul and spirit to incarnate in a healthy way into a physical body. The human individuality is understood to be eternal in Waldorf education, and prior to conception and birth to be in the guardianship of the spiritual world. Through birth, as Rudolf Steiner puts it, "the human being descends, as it were, as Spirit-Soul or Soul-Spirit into earthly existence. It cloaks itself with earthly existence."

In *The Foundations of Human Experience*,[9] a course of fourteen lectures that Rudolf Steiner gave to the first Waldorf teachers, he states unequivocally, "The task of education, understood in a spiritual sense, is to bring the soul-spirit into harmony with the temporal body. They must be brought into harmony, and they must be tuned to one another because when the child is born into the physical world, they do not yet properly fit each other. The task of the teacher is to harmonize these two parts to one another."[10] This harmonization process begins at birth and continues into adulthood. It centrally involves parents and teachers as the guardians of the emerging individuality.

The first phase of this harmonization process occurs in the preschool years and is ideally devoted to providing a safe, healthy and loving environment in which the physical body can unfold in such a way that it can carry the soul and spiritual potential of the growing child. A safe and loving environment is the basis for confidence and creativity in later life, and an environment worthy of imitation in speech, rhythm, color, form and mood can offer the first experience of the truly human. The power of imitation is great, as parents notice when their four-year-old faithfully mimics their habits. I remember changing the diapers of my young daughter and looking down to see her sticking out her tongue, a replica of my own gesture when faced with a demanding task.

It is also in these early years that standing, the development of language, and the use of "I" occurs, giving the young child the basis of its unique human existence. In Waldorf preschools and kindergartens the need for play, safety and an environment worthy of imitation are honored so that the important activity of developing the physical instrument, the body, can take place in a healthy manner. In the first seven years, Waldorf education recognizes that young children still carry with them an echo of their spiritual past, and that they believe the world is good. Rudolf Steiner suggests, "Children are beings that still believe in the morality of the world, and therefore believe they may imitate the world. It is precisely this which is so uplifting and wonderful about them."[11]

If in the first seven years children live in the afterglow of the past, in the second they live fully in the present. This period can rightly be described as the heart of childhood, not only because it is the middle period of childhood, but also because it is during this time that the feeling life of the child is developed. It is also during this time that the formative forces initially active in the head and the forces of "awakeness" that animated the young child in its limbs meet in the rhythmic system of the heart and lungs. A.C. Harwood notes, "It is an age of free rhythmical movement. Jumping, skipping, hopping, swinging their legs as they sit on the high adult chairs, running as naturally as they walk, the children exercise their rhythmic powers in almost everything they do."[12] Working with rhythm, and out of the caring adult authority of the class teacher, a sense of wonder and reverence for the world can be fostered. This is difficult in the age of videos, computer games and the wisecrack. But a sense of reverence and an eye for beauty provide a basis for the development of the life or etheric body during the second cycle of seven years. If we as Waldorf teachers and parents can provide an experience of the goodness and morality of the world in the first seven years, and foster a reverence for beauty in the second, we lay the foundation for physical and psychological health in adulthood.

As the child enters adolescence, ever earlier in a culture that pushes children into adulthood and consumption, a marked change occurs both in physical maturity and in individual consciousness. A central insight of Rudolf Steiner's about childhood development is that the child grows from the head down and awakens from the bottom up. The young child's head and nerve system develop first, then its rhythmic system and lastly, in adolescence, its limb system with the ability to reproduce its own kind. An opposite movement of "awakeness" occurs, starting in the limbs, the body of the baby in which it senses everything; then to the heart-lung system in the time between 7 and 14, expressed in the development of feelings; and then coming to self-awareness and a new cognitive capacity of consciousness in the head during adolescence. Harwood describes adolescence as the climax of the process of incarnation. "The child achieves the last physical accomplishment, the ability to reproduce its kind. In nothing is the human being more different from the animal than in the results of puberty—in the animal, maturity and absorption into his species; in man, the beginning of new mental powers and the appearance of unsuspected traits of individuality. But, physically speaking, the child stands on the earth at puberty, a mature member of the human race."[13]

A high school teacher and friend once remarked to me that adolescence is a building site with a sign saying, "Under Construction." Sometimes you see a child, sometimes an adult, and often you don't have a clue which of the two you are dealing with. What is fully visible are the awkward and painful attempts to find one's own individuality, a new sense of self and a new perceptive and cognitive capacity for understanding the world. If in early childhood a sense for the goodness of the world has been given and in the middle years of childhood a sense of beauty developed, then in the high school years a love for the world and for the truth and lawfulness of history, science, and art can be nurtured. It is a time in which "conception" as an individual cognitive and reproductive capacity becomes available, and a future orientation towards life as an adult manifests.

In our culture, the young person is considered an adult at twenty-one. This awareness mirrors the understanding of the human being embodied in Waldorf education, because at around twenty-one, the individuality of the person—the ego—is seen as connecting more deeply to the physical, life and soul body that has been prepared through childhood and adolescence. It is the task of Waldorf education, and of teachers and parents as guardians of the emerging individuality, to make this process of incarnation as harmonious as possible so that each child can become a free, morally responsible and creative individual.

The Mysteries of Human Encounter and Karma

Every Waldorf school is a destiny community, meaning that there is an intentional quality that brings a group of children, teachers and parents together to start a new school, or a group of seventeen children and a forty-year-old class teacher together to form a third grade. This intentional quality of relationships in Waldorf schools is seen as a reflection of a pre-birth intention that brings a specific group of children and parents together with a specific group of teachers and staff. Before turning to the objections that these statements can naturally raise, let me briefly elaborate the underlying perspective given by Rudolf Steiner, which permeates much of Waldorf education.

Every human being goes through repeated earth lives, gaining in experience, consciousness and insight. At the end of life, we shed our physical body, go through a short review or retrospective of our life and give up our soul body before journeying through the spiritual world, reviewing and digesting our life. This review is objective in the sense that we experience ourselves as others have experienced our thoughts, feelings and deeds. We then distill this learning in our higher self or ego, and make the resolve to incarnate again. Then begins the journey to incarnation, weaving a tapestry of life intentions together with our destiny partners: those parents and siblings, these key experiences, that class teacher, those colleagues, partners, vocational opportunities and limitations. We are weaving a life plan that goes into our limbs when we are born, disappearing from consciousness, but taking us with unerring accuracy to be born in a particular town, or to a first meeting with a lifelong friend at a summer camp when we are fifteen. It may also give us the gift of Waldorf education or of a stern but wonderful fourth grade teacher in public school.

How can we know whether such a picture is true and not just a convenient fantasy? We can reflect on our own life experiences, our biography, to see if we can find clear patterns of destiny, from life themes and challenges to deep friendships, where even on our first meeting we have a sense of, "Oh, here you are at last! I've missed you and know you." If we are more philosophically oriented, we can see if the teachings of reincarnation and karma by Rudolf Steiner or others make sense or add depth and perspective to the basic questions of the meaning of life.[14] Why am I a woman or a Chinese-American now? Why did this accident occur when I was twenty-four? Why do I have a fascination with Egyptian culture? In my experience, the perspective and, I believe, truth of reincarnation and karma empower us, help us to take responsibility for our lives and guide us in the direction of trying to learn our central lessons in this incarnation.

While there is no conclusive proof of reincarnation and karma, there is a growing body of personal and empirical evidence to support it. Recently I ran across two interesting and compelling books: *Old Souls: The Scientific Evidence for Past Lives* by Tom Schroder, which examines the extraordinarily detailed research of Dr. Ian Stevenson about children's recollections of previous incarnations, and *Expecting Adam* by Martha Beck, a remarkable account of her spiritual experiences with her light-filled, joyous, handicapped son.[15]

Given that Waldorf school communities are permeated with a sense that each school is a destiny community of children, teachers, parents, and staff, how does this mystery come to manifestation? Central is the long-term relationship between the class teacher and the individual child, a relationship acknowledged every day through a handshake, through the sense of responsibility the teacher feels for each child's well-being and through the individual inner meditative work the teacher does in thinking about and picturing his or her class.

Another aspect of this sense for mutual destiny is the commitment made by Waldorf school teachers and staff to working through their issues with children, colleagues and parents—to see each encounter as an opportunity for growth and learning. While this work is not always successful, sometimes failing because of limited skill or commitment, it is fundamental to the working of a Waldorf school community. As previously suggested, the intensity of working relationships in Waldorf schools gives each of us an opportunity to meet our untransformed sides, our shadow, while at the same time offering us the possibility of learning to care and to love. The recognition that we are destiny partners in the school is fostered by the collegial, non-hierarchical nature of decision making and the partnership between teachers, parents and staff for the sake of the children.

There is another aspect to the mystery of human encounter and karma that Rudolf Steiner describes. He suggests that, in the future, all human meetings, all encounters will acquire a sacramental quality.[16] We have an inkling of this already in those moments of grace when we experience something of the spiritual essence of another. This experience of grace and mutual blessing through human meeting will become so strong and so clearly an experience of soul and spirit that it will replace the role of the church as an opportunity of worship. To practice the sacramental qualities of conversation and encounter is another of those opportunities offered to us by Waldorf schools and other spiritually-grounded collegial institutions. It is the surest way of moving toward the ideals of peace and mutual understanding and support which we all long for.

The Mysteries of Family and Community Life

Now we come again to a question that has been at the heart of our reflections in this book: How can we as individuals create families and communities that honor the human being, the spirit and the earth? We began our journey by noting that the humanly created world—the world of conversations, families, shops, schools, towns and nations—is increasingly replacing the natural world as the main focus of our experience.[17] We have become like gods, creating a new world, a new universe, with the power of enhancing or destroying life. Atomic energy, gene manipulation and the world of artificial intelligence and cyberspace are the most dramatic expressions of this new power and responsibility. But it is the realm of the everyday—the family, school and community—that provides the basic practice ground for our social creativity and responsibility.

We have explored the intentional and karmic nature of family and school life. This foundational orientation can lead us to take all relational life seriously and to practice care, consciousness and the values of stewardship toward our partners and our children, and toward the other members of our work and school communities. This is particularly true of our relationship to our children. Like teachers, we are guardians of their health and development, needing to be ever- mindful of the great task we have in helping them to realize their potential, not our potential. As children grow into adolescence, their friends and their interests begin to significantly diverge from ours. Will we support the at-times-painful exploration of this growing independence or insist on our values, our truths and our career choices?

Waldorf schools support a deeper understanding of this guardian or stewardship role of parents in many ways. By providing an image of child development, and by providing parents with insights into the developmental needs, challenges, and opportunities of a three-, nine- or fourteen-year-old, Waldorf education helps to awaken a deeper interest in us about the nature of childhood and the unique character of each individual child.

While relationships and family life are the most basic building blocks of our society, our culture does little to support either. Waldorf schools provide a conscious counterweight by fostering a new, child-centered education and the possibility of a new family culture.

If approached consciously, building families, schools and communities can be seen as a modern form of temple building. Families, like schools and indeed all institutions, have a biography, a history, and they have a body, a soul and a spirit. For a family, the body is the home environment; the soul is the particular quality of moods, rituals, and the nature of relationships between family members; while the spirit is the being, the angel or deva that carries and inspires the family through time. Waldorf education actively supports family culture by placing an emphasis on the beauty and appropriateness of the physical environment. It supports the soul life by emphasizing yearly festivals and the importance of daily rituals such as baking, gardening and a common meal. It also supports the soul life through encouraging music, art and conversation as shared activities in the home. Furthermore, it makes possible a community of support among families, creating a forum where issues of television, designer clothes, discipline and slow reading can be explored.

Waldorf schools also nurture the spiritual life of families by pointing to the relevance of reverence, prayer, and inner development and to the need for common celebrations—birthdays, anniversaries and festivals. It is through such activities that we provide sustenance to the being of the family and refresh ourselves. For Waldorf schools, supporting family life is a vital though secondary goal in educating the children. Groups such as the Alliance for Childhood and Lifeways have made this a central priority. It can also become an important focus for the parent association.[18]

Supporting the development of a new, more conscious family culture is a vital need of our time and is the essential basis for a quality education. Schools can only provide a context for this renewed emphasis on family life, but the work of supporting and enriching home and relationships must come from the parents themselves. To recognize the sacramental nature of relationships, of having children and building a home and family, is a beginning. To share the struggles and learnings of building families consciously as communities is a new and vital work for the future.

If homes and families are the primary practice ground of our social creativity and responsibility, then schools and other organizations are a close second, as working adults spend over sixty percent of their waking time at work. All organizations are a web of relationships. An important condition of honoring our responsibilities in the social creation process is to foster those organizational and community forms that encourage the interests, participation and responsibility of the stakeholders in our institutions. All organizations and communities are partnerships— in the case of schools, partnerships between teachers, parents, administration and community for the education of children.

If building communities and organizations is to be approached consciously, it is important to recognize, as we have seen, that organizations, like all human beings and families, have a body, soul and spirit. The body can be seen as the building, machines, technology and work process; the soul as the qualities and values expressed in relationships, both internal and external; and the spirit as the unique mission and biography of each institution.

More than that, institutions are expressions of human psychological and spiritual qualities and in all cases are abodes for spiritual beings. Indeed, organizations of all kinds are the modern equivalent of the sacred groves of ancient times. They are the places where the gods now live and work. Positive working spirit beings want to co-create the social world with human beings. Our part in this co-creation process is to see that the community or institution stays in development and has a healthy body, soul and spirit.

Clarifying how your school or community serves human needs is a way of enlivening the spirit. What is its central mission and what are its main goals? This can be done through a clear articulation of the principles of Waldorf pedagogy, through long-term planning, a future search process or through periodic reviews of where you are and where you want to go. A central quality of any such process is to see it as an offering to the human and spiritual communities the institution serves, and therefore to invite your parents, clients or stakeholders into the process.

Another way of reconnecting to an organization's spiritual identity is to celebrate the institution's history—its tenth anniversary or its fiftieth—or to create a myth or story that expresses your school's journey. Sharing verses, important thoughts or aspirations among colleagues also enlivens your sense of purpose and is a source of nourishment to the spiritual world. Perhaps most important in nourishing the spiritual identity of Waldorf schools is a living, shared child and pedagogical study.

The soul life in schools and other organizations is expressed in the quality of formal and informal relationships, in policies and in the nature of leadership and decision making. Is there trust? Are difficulties worked through openly? Is decision making transparent? To consciously work on the soul life in Waldorf schools means assessing the state of the school as a community. It means articulating the principles and forms of governance in a governance plan so that the nature of the partnership between teachers, parents, Board and administrative staff is clear and mutually understood.

Another way of shaping the soul life of a group or school is to articulate the expectations we have of each other in our relationships as principles to practice. In faculty meetings, for example, this could mean being on time, coming prepared, listening and participating actively, seeking common ground, respecting confidentiality, making decisions through consensus and learning through group review. Agreements around such practices can be used periodically to review meetings: How are we doing with these practices? What is working well? Where do we need to put more emphasis?

Common celebrations and events that don't have a functional agenda are another important part of the formation of the soul life of all institutions. Once when I was doing some work with a College council and faculty, we all went bowling. The resulting hilarity and good feeling still live in the collective memory, years after the event. In the Threefold Community in Spring Valley, New York, where I lived for many years, there are occasional all-community dances and events in which people of all ages participate, from sixth graders to grandparents. These activities nurture relationships through having fun together.

Turning to the body of the school or community, Waldorf schools are increasingly able to acquire or build school buildings that reflect the educational philosophy and values of the pedagogy. The San Francisco Waldorf School, The City of Lakes Waldorf School in Minneapolis, the Hartsbrook School in Hadley, Massachusetts, and the Pine Hill School in Wilton, New Hampshire, all have quite different buildings, but each school is able to express its identity and values in meaningful ways and to create a beautiful and harmonious environment worthy of the education. Furthering the Waldorf building impulse is important work that is, fortunately, being supported by the Rudolf Steiner Foundation and other individuals and groups.

To my mind, buildings are not the only manifestation of the limb system or body of the school. The work and administrative life also belong, in part, to this realm. Previously, we have looked at fostering the values of service and competence in the life of the school. Having clear administrative structures and procedures, delegating responsibilities to groups and individuals based on competence, is both an opportunity and a challenge.

Reading the Books of Nature and Civilization

The next two mysteries celebrated in Waldorf education are strongly rooted in the curriculum of the twelve grades. In describing the esoteric background of Waldorf education, René Querido suggests that the curriculum can be divided into two main parts: learning to read in the book of nature and understanding the book of civilization or the history of human activity.[19] The first involves developing a living relationship to the kingdoms of nature, to the living earth, to farming and craft activity and increasingly from grade five on to the natural sciences. Understanding the book of history is fostered through a gradual unfolding of the sweep of human history using a strongly biographical approach so that children experience not only the evolving consciousness of human beings as it connects to their own changing sensibilities, but also can identify with the struggles and accomplishments of great personalities.

In the first grade, fairy stories and folk tales mirror the evolving consciousness of the child. Fairy tales from older times are important because they contain an ancient wisdom, "the moral lessons and practical wisdom of our ancestors," as Harwood puts it.[20] Older fairy tales, whether European, Celtic, Chinese or African, are supplemented in the second grade by fables such as Aesop's and by legends, which lead children from the archetypal world to the perception of more human qualities in nature and in the human being's relationship to nature.[21]

In the third grade, Old Testament stories—Noah with the animals and David and Goliath—supplemented by historical legends from other traditions, such as the Native American, present a picture of the human being's descent from innocence, the fall from Paradise. Being busy with this imaginative content in art—painting, modeling, movement and the making of main lesson books—deepens memory and creates a sense for beauty.

In the third grade, reading the book of nature is experienced in the farming block, the caring for animals and living with the seasonal cycles of nature: planting, nurturing and harvesting crops. The building block in the third grade encompasses not only the making of shelters, but exploring the construction of houses from many different materials: igloos, adobe structures and reed huts. This gives a picture and an experience of how what is received from nature, from the gods, is transformed by human activity into the basic necessities of life: food and shelter.

In the fourth grade, local history and geography are added, with map-making and exploration along with the creation stories of Norse mythology in which the gods have most human failings.

We can see that in being introduced to the book of nature, we begin to move into the sciences: botany in fifth grade; mineralogy in the sixth grade; mechanics, physics and astronomy in seventh; and chemistry and physiology in eighth. In these four years, the children are also introduced to the great sweep of civilization from ancient India, Persia and Egypt in fifth grade through Rome, Christianity and the Middle Ages in sixth, the birth of the Renaissance and the Age of Discovery in seventh, through the Revolutions of the 18th century up to the present time in the eighth grade.

Rudolf Steiner captured the essences of the Waldorf curriculum by saying that education should be nurturing for young children, enlivening in the middle grades and awakening in the high school.[22]

In an overview of the curriculum edited by Martyn Rawson and Tobias Richter, the central task of the upper school is described as helping young people experience the question: "What do I need to do to be useful to society?"[23] This involves helping young people discover their individuality, deepen their powers of observation and judgment, develop a moral and ethical sense, acquire skills and competencies in a variety of subjects and become actively engaged with the world and its challenges. What was presented more imaginatively in the lower grades and artistically in the middle school is now presented out of the phenomena, with more emphasis on the individual student's interpretation and understanding.

In the ninth grade, modern history is again the focus with a thorough examination of the industrial, technological and social revolutions of the 19th and 20th centuries. The achievements and challenges of the modern age are worked with. In the sciences, mineralogy, meteorology and the beginnings of organic chemistry are taught.

A recapitulation of historical evolution takes place between the tenth and twelfth grades, starting with ancient cultures in the tenth and ending with a look at modern economic and political systems in the twelfth. In the sciences, chemistry and biochemistry, physiology, physics, botany and increasingly complex mathematics are taught from tenth grade on so that at graduation, the student has a living relationship not only to the earth, but also to the analytical, technological world of modern science and mathematics.

Outlining the curriculum, of course, does not do justice to how the subject main lessons are taught nor does it reveal the underlying imaginations living in the education which can help to make reading the book of nature and the book of civilization sacramental, something both awe-inspiring and life-affirming. Perhaps I can go back to an activity described in the first chapter, by way of analogy. If we light candles before a meal, the soul effect will be quite different from that of a quickly thrown-together meal eaten on a table filled with daily clutter. If children are first introduced to the wonders of nature imaginatively, and see that the gifts of nature are gifts from the gods as portrayed in ancient myths and legends, and then experience how human beings shape these gifts of the mineral, plant and animal kingdoms through agriculture, art and crafts, then they will have a different inner relationship to the world when they work with the disciplines of modern science in high school. They will have a sense that nature is the face of a great Being and that humanity needs to be a responsible steward of what it has been given. Without such an inner orientation fostered by the curriculum in the lower and middle school, nature and the world can be seen as a storehouse to be plundered or desecrated to support our lifestyle choices.

In coming to a deeper understanding of history, of the story of civilization, a similar choice is evident. One of the experiences I had while working at Sunbridge College was meeting many students who had a limited sense of history and who hated the process of memorizing dates and facts. For them, the history curriculum was not the unfolding of the great journey of humanity from a state of dependency, of living in the lap of the gods, to increasing independence and responsibility in the course of millennia. Nor were they ignited by the adventures of Odysseus, the greatness of Alexander or the musings of Copernicus. In Waldorf schools, history is a joyous and exciting affair in which the evolution of humanity, from a collective consciousness connected to the cycles of nature to the individualized self-consciousness of the present, is celebrated. The experience of this journey, enlivened by drama, literature and the arts not only gives the students a love of history, but confidence in the evolution of mankind and a positive orientation toward their own lives. Learning to read in the book of nature and in the book of civilization are, therefore, two of the essential mysteries celebrated in Waldorf schools that provide the basis for a new culture.

Co-Creating with the Spirit

In 1923 Rudolf Steiner gave Ralph Courtney, an American reporter for the then-existing *New York Herald Tribune,* a meditation called the Threefold or America Verse previously alluded to:

> May our feeling penetrate into the center of our hearts
> And seek in love to unite itself with human beings sharing the same goals
> And with spirit beings who, bearing grace
> And strengthening us from realms of light
> And illuminating our love,
> Are gazing down upon our earnest, heartfelt striving.

The verse captures an essential aspect of our work in building Waldorf school communities: the ongoing creation process between human and spiritual beings.

Vaclav Havel points to the reality of this co-creation process when he calls for an awareness of the "secret order of the cosmos" and suggests the importance of assuming that we are beheld "from above."[24] When the teacher reflects on an individual child's needs and circumstances or when a group of teachers inwardly holds a child who has lost a parent, they are seeking to connect both to the child's soul and spirit and to the guardian angel of the child. As a class teacher prepares a lesson for the next day and thinks of what the class needs in order to better understand fractions, he or she seeks to gain guidance from spiritual beings who accompany the children and the whole class in its development. If this seeking of guidance is consciously connected to a question, then an insight, story or example is often given.

When a school community is facing a serious challenge, for example the need for a new home, and the College of Teachers and the Board ask for guidance from the Being of the school, then, in my experience, help is provided. Such assistance is seldom in the form of a grand illumination experienced by everyone, but comes rather in the form of a thought or phrase shared by a few people which resonates in the whole circle, or a phone call two days later to the school administrator describing a possible site no one had previously thought of.

Another frequently experienced dialog with spiritual beings I believe happens in the preschool when a class visits a rocky stream bed or builds stick houses in a pine forest. The children often relate that they saw a gnome or heard a water sprite, commenting in a matter of fact way on their natural awareness of nature spirits.[25]

This notion of co-creating with a host of spiritual beings may strike some as fanciful, but what is prayer and meditation but an effort to have a dialog with the spiritual ground of existence. The difference is that in Steiner's work, as in many other spiritual traditions, there are a multitude of spiritual beings and forces actively engaged in helping to shape human and earth activity. So, the question of a dialog with the spirit becomes the questions: Which spirit, what type of dialog and how can we begin to discern guidance from the multitude of impressions we receive.

Rudolf Steiner's spiritual philosophy or cosmology is, of course, not taught as content in Waldorf schools, but the education is clearly based on spiritual images of the human being and of earth evolution. In building Waldorf school communities, we are asked to consider the possibility of a new, more conscious relationship to the angel of a child, the spirit of a family or the being of the school and we are invited to practice being in dialog with the spiritual world through festivals and a multitude of other school activities.

That we have limited skill and a limited understanding of this co-creation with spirit is no doubt true. Yet many teachers, parents and friends of Waldorf education share a sense that we are at a time in human evolution when a new conscious dialog with the spiritual world is not only possible but necessary. My own experience suggests that positive working spiritual beings and forces are most anxious to enter a new relationship with humanity or, as Marjorie Spock suggests, "the spiritual world beyond the threshold wishes every bit as keenly to be known as we wish to know it."[26] This requires that we develop a new sensitivity and consciously turn to the spiritual world for guidance and insight.

Quite a few years ago I was asked to give a talk at the New York Open Center, a large alternative adult education initiative in New York City, on "Working with Angels." I hesitated as this was not my usual fare in giving public presentations. After some reflection, I agreed and spent a beautiful autumn afternoon preparing. I had finished an outline and mentally said, "Well, what have I left out?" Almost immediately, a loud, deep and humorous voice said, "You have left out celebrating with us." I was shocked, turned around, but of course, no one was physically present. The voice was right and while I tried to ask further questions, this was all the help I was going to get.

The relationship to spiritual beings is complex. Even the notion of seeing angels and archangels as separate entities from us is too simple, as they inhabit spaces, live in institutions and dwell in our consciousness. Dr. Michael Abrams, an emergency room physician, relates angels saying, "We are you, the real you. If we get involved—and make no mistake about it, we do get involved in your lives—we do so as extensions of your own will. …When you think a thought or pray a prayer, …that thought goes out into the universe and begins to take form. You, spirit and all of Spirit's messengers and agents, all of us are connected together in one milieu, one gigantic coordinated field of consciousness."[27]

Another aspect of our relationship to spiritual beings is that there are beings that do not assist us in our journey toward greater freedom and responsibility. Rudolf Steiner refers to these beings as Luciferic and Ahrimanic beings, Luciferic beings who would have us glory in our beauty, creativity and automatic goodness ,and Ahrimanic spirits who would have us deny our spiritual nature and who support an egotistical, materialistic approach to life.[28] These spirits do not require our conscious participation to influence us. They do make our development possible by providing us with choices and resistances which make our evolution toward enhanced freedom possible. It is the beings who serve the time spirit, who serve the course of human evolution who are required to respect our freedom and who require our conscious participation if a dialog with spirit is to occur.

In reflecting on the mystery of our co-creation with Spirit, we also need to be aware that the dead have a great interest in what happens on earth. Many individuals are aware of the guidance, insight and reassuring presence coming from loved ones who are no longer on earth but who maintain an interest in our work and in institutions they were once connected to. Through honoring them and being aware of their presence and interest, we are also co-creating with spirit.[29]

In my work as an advisor to school communities, I am sometimes asked how we can make the dialog with spirit more conscious. I have described an approach at the end of this chapter under "Exercises."

The culture of Waldorf schools with its festivals, verses and sayings provides children with a mood of reverence for the spiritual dimension of life. And it provides teachers, parents and staff with an ongoing opportunity for conscious dialog with spiritual beings. To my mind, this is an opportunity which we haven't sufficiently exercised and doing so would help us in overcoming our one-sidedness and would serve to ameliorate the host of interpersonal issues which plague many self-administered, collegial institutions. To remember that we are beheld and that we serve human and spiritual beings is a bracing tonic for our own egotism.

In celebrating the mystery of co-creating with the spirit in Waldorf schools, we have the opportunity of celebrating a mystery which Rudolf Steiner describes in the following way, "commonly willed...human associations are the secret places where higher spiritual beings descend in order to work through individuals, just as the soul works through the members of the body."[30]

The Mystery of the Free Human Being

I have described six mysteries or sacraments which live within the many daily activities of a Waldorf school—in the morning verse, an artfully prepared main lesson, a faculty meeting, a festival or a conversation with a concerned parent. These mysteries include the process of human incarnation and development contained in the image of child development, the mystery of human encounter and karma, the mystery of family and community life, the twin mysteries of reading the book of nature and the book of history, which together form the heart of the curriculum, and the mystery of co-creating with the spirit. The seventh mystery is the mystery of the free human being, by which I mean the possibility of becoming a more conscious, moral and loving person through the practice of self-development, of inner development and self-transformation. It is both the basis and the culmination of what can make Waldorf education a temple for bringing the sacred into daily life, for connecting spirit and matter.

The practice of inner development, of self-transformation can only be self-chosen and worked on by the individual. It can be supported by the community, but in the end it must be done through daily and weekly practice. Self-awareness, social understanding, compassion and moral insight are not a birthright nor are they qualities fostered by the materialistic consumer societies of the West. Yet without our taking steps to foster our soul and spiritual development, we have neither the possibility of increased freedom, suffering from what Buddhists refer to as excessive attachment, nor the possibility of creating healthy relationships and new communities.

In my experience, the overwhelming majority of adults in Waldorf school communities are committed to inner work and are looking for the spiritual in the process of education and community life. If seventy-nine percent of Americans describe themselves as more spiritual than religious (and are looking for "transcendence in the midst of the mundane"), then the percentage of Waldorf school teachers, parents and staff sharing this orientation is still higher.[31] Could we, should we not then express the expectation in Waldorf schools that all adult members of the community are on a self-chosen path of reflection and inner growth? By this I do not mean that all adults in Waldorf schools should be students of Rudolf Steiner or anthroposophy, although this is advisable for teachers since they work on a daily basis with the image of child development and the many aspects of the curriculum which he initially developed. All adults in Waldorf schools should, however, be committed to self-reflection and inner growth; otherwise the new community forms practiced in Waldorf education are not sustainable. I have worked in some schools where personality conflicts, disagreements about aspects of decision making or groups wishing to gain power can create a climate of such suspicion and enmity that the school is unable to function. Partnership forms are very vulnerable to such disruptions unless, in thought and deed, the adult members of the community attempt to work with the best in themselves and others, to recognize that schools are destiny communities in which we are partners in mutual development.

When I mention a self-chosen path of inner development, I mean a path which shares the principles found in all spiritual traditions. Whether Christian, Buddhist, Hindu, Jewish or Muslin, the great spiritual and religious traditions of humanity share three essential qualities. The first of these is reverence and gratitude for the earth and for the miracle of human life. The second could be called the practice of mindfulness, of educating the soul to bring greater consciousness to outer and inner experiences, while the third quality is a dialog with the divine, with the spiritual world, through prayer and meditation.

Practicing reverence and gratitude establishes a basic soul mood which Rudolf Steiner described as essential for connecting us to life and the world around us. He remarked, "We advance even more quickly [on the path of inner development] if, in such moments [of inner reflection] we fill our consciousness with admiration, respect and reverence for the world and for life."[32]

Mindfulness activities are exercises to educate and direct our soul faculties of thinking, feeling and willing so that we enhance our capacities to experience ourselves and the world more consciously. We all have the experience of beginning to think about a question—say, the beauty of autumn leaves or a meeting with a friend two days from now—and before we know it, we are reflecting on the need to pay bills or the upcoming Labor Day picnic. It is the same with our feelings:

hearing someone make a remark and being quickly annoyed without knowing why or a momentary gush of enthusiasm because we have been praised. In the area of our will, following our conscious intention, our ability to direct our actions is even more precarious. The question we each face on a daily basis is whether we are thought, felt and willed through outer circumstances or have some measure of direction and control over our attention and behavior.

For Rudolf Steiner there were certain conditions which needed to be met for a path of inner development to be healthy and grounded in the realities of life. For him this meant practicing clear thinking, focused will, equanimity, positivity and open-mindedness, and working with these five in harmony. These exercises for educating thinking, feeling and willing are sometimes called the subsidiary or complementary exercises.

The first, control of thinking, involves placing an ordinary object in your consciousness—say, a button or a paper clip—and focusing on it exclusively for five minutes or more. What is its function, of what is it made, how is it manufactured, and so on. It is suggested to work on this for a week or a month and then add the will exercise to do a non-functional deed at a certain time every day—say, removing your left shoe at 3:15 or shifting your watch from one wrist to the other.

The practice of equanimity is recommended next so that we are not too strongly affected by ordinary events, moved to great fluctuations of joy or sorrow, but are able to observe our feelings. The fourth exercise involves developing positivity, looking for the good, the beautiful in all things and all people without thereby denying that which is difficult. The practice of this exercise is subtle for it asks us to move behind our automatic likes and dislikes to a deeper feeling of beholding. Open-mindedness, the fifth exercise, is ever more difficult as we get older. Think of the young child's delight with every new experience. Can we cultivate an ongoing openness to new truths, new insights and new experiences? Working with these five exercises regularly, making them a habit to be worked on through the day, the week and the year, gives us a certain soul stability and flexibility which is health-giving.[33]

The eightfold path of Buddha contains a well-established set of mindfulness exercises for educating the soul quite similar to Steiner's activities. These practices include: Right Judgment, to uncover and bring to consciousness the motives and reasons for a decision; Right Word, bringing thoughtfulness to our speech and conversation; Right Deed, bringing awareness to our actions and their consequences; Right Standpoint, ordering our life in accordance with nature and the spirit; Right Memory, the effort to learn as much as possible from life through reflection and conscious observation; Right Opinion, paying attention to one's thinking and distinguishing between essential and non-essential in the search for truth; Right Examination, in moments of quiet to take counsel with oneself to test and form the principles of one's life; and lastly, to let these exercises Become a Habit in daily life.[34] The Buddha gave the eightfold path as a set of practices to his disciples and to humanity as part of his teachings on love and compassion, as a way of overcoming pain and suffering in the world.

While mindfulness exercises vary between individuals and also between spiritual traditions, they share the aim of educating awareness. Recently, in a small group of seven students exploring questions of inner development, I noted over forty practices, ranging from conscious speaking and listening to nature observation, concentration exercises, creating daily moments of silence, walking with awareness, attending to breathing, an evening review of the day, listening to sounds and looking for a conscious miracle each day.

Building on the six mindfulness exercises described by Rudolf Steiner, Michael Lipson, in his excellent short book, *Stairway of Surprise*, notes, "This most fundamental human capacity—the capacity to attend—is the human extra. It can be strengthened so that we apply ourselves more creatively to our chosen work and play, regaining something of the small child's total immersion."[35]

Having worked on our soul development through mindfulness activities, we are in a position to consider prayer and meditation as complementary ways of addressing the spirit. Prayer is fundamentally "an upward gaze of the soul from the transitory present into the eternal that embraces past, present and future." It must be free of selfish motives so that it can be "a cry to the divine to come to us and fill us with its power."[36] Whatever its form and irrespective of religious tradition, true payer leads to a recognition that we are all connected, part of the divine world, and can accept the past and trust the future.

If prayer is a petition to the divine world to be present in our life, then meditation is an effort to raise our consciousness to the spiritual world, through using non-material images and thoughts to attain spiritual insight. "When we raise ourselves through meditation to what unites us with the spirit, we quicken something within us that is external and unlimited by birth and death."[37] In meditating on a profound thought or phrase: "In the beginning was the Word, and the Word was with God and the Word was God,"[38] or the Hindu saying: "Man habitually identifies the Self with the non-Self," or an insightful poem or sacred image, we attempt to raise our consciousness into a spirit beholding.

In so doing, we become aware that we are spiritual beings, with spiritual capacities and the ability to gain wisdom. For Rudolf Steiner the path of reverence, the practice of mindfulness, provides a basis for spiritual cognition, and meditation leads to an unfolding of this capacity. As he stated in the beginning of *How to Know Higher Worlds*, "The capacities by which we gain insights into higher worlds lie dormant within each of us."[39] The challenge is to unfold these capacities through practice.

Of course, we recognize that as we grow older there is a process of maturation, of development in life. We can enhance this learning by consciously reflecting on our biography, on our life lessons. Then we can begin a process of soul and spirit development; we can go a path of inner transformation through the practice of gratitude and reverence, mindfulness, and prayer and meditation. To do so, I believe, provides the essential basis of all new communities and of new, more equitable, sustainable societies. Going a path of inner development is the substance of the mystery of the free human being because we must choose it anew each day and because, when practiced, it provides a growing sense of freedom and responsibility for the human being.

I have suggested that we can find three levels of activity on the path of inner development within all spiritual traditions. First is gratitude or remembering what the spiritual world has given: our life, our food and the physical instrument to experience the world, our body. Second is mindfulness activities in order to educate our soul so that it is able to attend, to be aware of the reality of soul and spirit now, both internally and externally. The third level is then prayer and meditation as a way of directing our gaze to the spirit, of spirit beholding. Rudolf Steiner captured these distinctions most beautifully in a lengthy meditation called the "Foundation Stone Meditation," which he shared with the delegates and members of the General Anthroposophical Society at the founding ceremony of this society between Christmas and New Year 1923–1924. This meditation consists of three great calls to the human soul:

Human Soul: Practice Spirit Remembering

This first call – Practice Spirit Remembering – is a call to develop gratitude and reverence for what has been given out of the past: our life, our body, our Earth. It is experienced through our limbs which bear us through the world of space. This gift of life has been given to us by the divine world and lives within our will system.

Human Soul: Practice Spirit Mindfulness

The second call – Practice Spirit Mindfulness – is a call to spirit awareness in the stream of time, to our process of becoming in life.

Human Soul: Practice Spirit Beholding

The third call – Practice Spirit Beholding in quietness of thought – is a call to truly think so that the thoughts of worlds and the eternal aims of gods are revealed to us.

Through working with this meditation, and in practicing Spirit Remembering (gratitude, reverence), Spirit Mindfulness (mindfulness activities) and Spirit Beholding (prayer and mediation), we may know ourselves more deeply and experience ourselves as part of an increasingly conscious and free humanity.[40]

I have attempted to articulate what I believe to be the mysteries which lie within the activities and forms of Waldorf education in the hope that others may reflect on and articulate these mysteries further. For Waldorf schools to realize their potential for the future, these mysteries must be practiced so that Waldorf education can become an ark, can become a cathedral for a new spiritually-aware age, an age in which humanity will be a responsible co-creator with the gods. I believe it is only when we are able to practice these sacramental qualities in everyday life and fill such activities with a new understanding, that we will be able to create a more equitable, sustainable society for the future, for then we will have a true education for ourselves and for our children.

Chapter VIII Exercises:

What follows are some thoughts about conditions that are important to keep in mind for individual or group dialog with spiritual beings. However, it is important for every person to find his or her method,:the approach and the practice of such conversations.

1) Create a quiet mood of reverence and expectancy.

2) Create a mood of trust and harmony.

3) Be clear that your motives are to serve a child, a colleague, a situation or a school.

4) Let go of your own pre-existing judgments about solutions or outcomes.

5) Ask a specific question of a specific being such as the "good spirit of this school" or "angel of this child," help us to find the right home or the right step for this particular child. If working in a group, agree beforehand on the question and the being to be addressed by each person.

6) Live in attentiveness for a thought, a phrase, a gesture or an image that appears in your emptied consciousness. Be patient and live in the stillness. Be aware that often answers may come from the outside in a letter, a phone call or a chance encounter days or even weeks after the question has been asked.

7) In discerning the truth of an answer, develop a sense for the unexpected and then weigh it against your understanding. If in a circle of colleagues, listen carefully to the impressions shared by each person and see what lights up for you and others.

8) Give thanks for help given, as it is all too easy to forget showing gratitude to the beings that accompany us on our journey or that live with us in the developing school community.

Endnotes

1. Richard Tarnas, *The Passion of the Western Mind* (Harmony Books, New York, 1991), p. 169.
2. Painton Cowen, *Rose Windows* (Thames and Hudson, London, 1974), pp. 12–13.
3. Kenneth Clark, *Civilization* (Harper and Row, London and New York, 1969), p. 56.
4. Gottfried Richter, *Art and Human Consciousness* (SteinerBooks, Great Barrington, MA, 1985), p. 132.
5. Emile Mâle, *The Gothic Image: Religious Art in France of the 13th Century* (Harper Torchbook, New York, 1958). This excellent work describes in detail how "the highest conception of theologian and scholar penetrated…the minds of even the humblest of people through the Art of the Cathedral." (Preface, vii).
6. Robert Forman, *Grassroots Spirituality* (Imprint Academic, Exeter, UK, 2004).
7. See Rex Raab and Arne Klingborg, *Die Waldorfschule baut, Sechstig Jahre Architektur der Waldorfschule* (Verlag Freies Geistesleben, Stuttgart, 1982).
8. See Rudolf Steiner, *The Child's Changing Consciousness as the Basis of Pedagogical Practice* (Anthroposophic Press, Hudson, NY, 1996). Also Roy Wilkinson, *The Spiritual Basis of Steiner Education* (Rudolf Steiner Press, London, 1996), E.A. Stockmeyer, *Rudolf Steiner's Curriculum for Waldorf Schools* (Rudolf Steiner Press, London, 1969), and A.C. Harwood, *The Recovery of Man in Childhood* (Hodden and Stoughton, London, 1958).
9. Rudolf Steiner, *The Foundations of Human Experience* (Anthroposophic Press, Hudson, NY, 1996), p. 39.
10. Ibid.
11. Ibid., p. 156.
12. Op. cit., Harwood, p. 72.
13. Ibid., p. 170.
14. Rudolf Steiner, *Manifestations of Karma* (Rudolf Steiner Press, London).
15. Tom Schroder, *Old Souls: The Scientific Evidence for Past Lives* (Simon and Schuster, NY, 1999). Martha Beck, *Expecting Adam: A True Story of Birth, Rebirth and Everyday Magic* (Random House, NY, 2000).
16. Rudolf Steiner, *The Work of the Angels in Man's Astral Body*, (Anthroposophic Press, Spring Valley, NY, 1985).
17. See Chapter I, pp. 1–12.
18. www.allianceforchildhood.org and www.lifewaysnorthamerica.org.
19. René Querido, *The Esoteric Background of Waldorf Education: The Cosmic Christ Impulse* (Rudolf Steiner College Press, Fair Oaks, CA, 1995), p. 26.
20. Op. cit., Harwood, p. 98.

21. Ibid., p. 98.

22. Op. cit., Querido, p. 36.

23. Martyn Rawson and Tobias Richter, *The Educational Tasks and Content of the Steiner Waldorf Curriculum* (Steiner Waldorf Schools Fellowship, Forest Row, England), p. 52.

24. Vaclav Havel, *Summer Meditations* (Alfred A. Knopf, New York, 1992), p. 6.

25. See Marko Pogacnik, *Nature Spirits and Elemental Beings* (Findhorn Press, Forres, Scotland, 1995).

26. Marjorie Spock, *The Art of Goethean Conversation* (St. George Publications, Spring Valley, NY; now available at Rudolf Steiner College Press, Fair Oaks, CA), p. 5.

27. Michael Abrams, *The Evolution Angel: An Emergency Physician's Lessons with Death and the Divine* (Abundance Media, Boulder, CO, 2000), pp. 66–67.

28. See Rudolf Steiner, "Lucifer and Ahriman," five lectures given in November 1919 (Steiner Book Centre, North Vancouver, BC, Canada, 1976).

29. Rudolf Steiner, *Staying Connected: How to Continue Your Relationships with Those Who Have Died* (Anthroposophic Press, Hudson, NY, 2002), pp. 26–27.

30. Rudolf Steiner, *Brotherhood and the Struggle for Existence* (Mercury Press, Spring Valley, NY, 1980), p. 9.

31. *Newsweek*, Sept. 5, 2005, pp. 48–52.

32. Rudolf Steiner, *How to Know Higher Worlds* (Anthroposophic Press, Great Barrington, MA, 2002), p. 20.

33. Rudolf Steiner, *Guidance in Esoteric Training* (Rudolf Steiner Press, London, 1977), pp. 13–19.

34. See Rudolf Steiner, *According to Luke* (Anthroposophic Press, Great Barrington, MA, 2001), pp. 70–80.

35. M. Lipson, *Stairway of Surprise: Six Steps to a Creative Life* (Anthroposophic Press, Great Barrington, MA, 2002), p. 10.

36. Rudolf Steiner, *Prayer* (Anthroposophic Press, Spring Valley, NY, 1977), pp. 12–13.

37. Op. cit., Steiner, *How to Know Higher Worlds*, p. 35.

38. *The Holy Bible*, King James version (Oxford University Press). The opening of the Gospel of St. John, Swami Prabhavaananda, *The Sermon on the Mount According to Vedanta* (Mentor Books, NY, 1963), p. 21.

39. Op. cit., Steiner, *How to Know Higher Worlds*, p. 13.

40. F.W. Zeylmans van Emmichoven (trans. George Adams), *The Foundation Stone* (Rudolf Steiner Press, London, 1963), pp. 6–29, slightly revised.

IX

An Education for Peace, for Hope and for the Social Future

We can learn to love not only what is, but what is to be.
                    – Bernard Lievegoed

When I think about our social future, I cannot see a positive outcome to the many social, economic, environmental and human challenges facing us unless human beings develop a new holistic and imaginative form of thinking, develop a deeper and more profound relationship to nature and become capable of a renewed dialog with each other and with the spirit. In my experience Waldorf education provides this opportunity to its graduates and offers hope for a peaceful and sustainable future.

In 1992 I attended a conference at Wainwright House in Rye, New York, in which sixteen educators wrestled with the topic of "The Renewal of Thinking in Education and Society." The lively discussions centered on how social change occurs and what the relationship is between the structures of consciousness—the prevailing mindset—and the structures of society. While participating in the conference I was also experiencing the gathering of fifty or so young people who met over three days to remember a dear young friend who had died in a tragic accident. In my heart these two events will always remain connected through the gift of being able to experience the love, insight and clarity with which this group of young people, mainly Waldorf graduates, celebrated and honored our friend. The two experiences also brought home to me the profound interconnection between consciousness and social forms, for I was experiencing a new form of celebrating a departed friend, not connected to religion or established rituals. It was being created in the moment by a new consciousness, a new heartfelt dialog within and between people and with the spirit.

Waldorf education both embodies a new educational consciousness which allows its graduates to experience and think about the world in new and imaginative ways, while at the same time fosters new institutional partnership forms, which have been described at length in these essays. Waldorf schools seek to educate children to become conscious, morally centered adults while practicing the social art of community building in their structures, processes and relationships.

When I meet Waldorf graduates, irrespective of their vocation and life circumstances, I am struck by their engagement with life and learning and their deep reverence for nature, people and the spirit. I think this is what Steiner was referring to when he said Waldorf education is an education for the future. Each generation of the young is the future, and if recent graduates have a strong sense of self, imaginative thinking, a love for the earth and each other and a commitment to learning and development, then they will bring healing to the world.

A strong sense of self and one's possibilities is the foundation for personal creativity and social engagement. Waldorf education fosters this dialog with the self, with the growing identity of the individual child in a myriad of ways, from honoring each child in the birthday celebrations of kindergarten to the handshake with the class teacher each morning, from the individually prepared notebooks for main lesson to the senior class projects. This leads to qualities often remarked upon by the friends and parents of Waldorf graduates: their trust and confidence in themselves and their desire to actively and creatively engage in the world.

Linked to a strong sense of one's own individuality is the ability to think imaginatively, to live with images which connect our objective and subjective experiences. For Douglas Sloan, the organizer of the previously mentioned educational conference in Rye, imagination is "experiencing thinking intensely as one's own, especially including one's own responsibility, and at the same time finding in it a bridge into universal intelligibility and reality. Moral imagination would then be integral to the same movement, a heightening and strengthening of one's own individuality until it becomes a window to what is universal to all humans."[1] This Waldorf education provides to its students.

A troubling aspect of much of modern education, and indeed of modern consciousness, is the loss of a living connection to nature. Strengthening the dialog of the human being with the natural world is an important aspect of Waldorf education. The relationship to the seasons, to plants and animals, to the elements of air, water, earth and fire is so integrated into the curriculum through festivals, gardening, crafts and art that a bridge is built to the wisdom and beauty of the natural world. Many Waldorf graduates I have talked to comment on the importance of their relation to nature as bringing healing and renewal to their lives and inspiration to their work. They also manifest a strong concern about environmental sustainability and a commitment to ecological ways of living.

I think of Waldorf education as an education for peace because, in my conflict resolution and community building work, I realize that resolving issues between individuals and groups requires the parties to recover the humanity of each other, moving from an "I–It" relation to an "I–Thou" relation, to use Martin Buber's phrase. It requires that individuals are self-reflective, have an interest in the other and are able and willing to learn from life. These are qualities Waldorf education strengthens while at the same time providing the ongoing practice of living in community with classmates, teachers and parents.

Peace also entails coming to an insight I had in my mid-twenties when studying international politics and economics: Violence and conflict exist not only between nations, groups and individuals, but also within myself. If my thoughts and feelings are real, then my negative, critical and destructive soul-state toward others or myself is the underpinning of violence and war in the world. As Edgar Cayce, renowned American psychic and healer, remarked, mind is the maker, or as Rudolf Steiner pointed out, unless we are willing to resolve conflicts and animosities within our own soul, there will be no peace in the world. Being able to engage in this kind of self-reflection in honesty requires moments of quiet and the ability to monitor our thoughts, feelings and behavior. This is not encouraged by the modern world, for it is potentially threatening to the established order. Yet it is an ability and a quality encouraged by Waldorf education and is wonderfully alive in the Waldorf graduates whom I have met.

An awareness of the spirit and the ability to have a dialog with spirit are grounded in this self-reflective consciousness. If we can perceive and monitor our thoughts, feelings and actions and if we have reverence for life and its gifts and challenges, then we are naturally led to the experiences of insight and of intuition. Experiencing an inner voice and recognizing that I can ask questions of the divine or of spiritual world is dialog with spirit. A sense for this inner dialog is strong in many Waldorf graduates who naturally access this inner way of knowing and are surprised when asked about it as it seems natural and vital to their way of being.

Waldorf education gives its students an experience of the world, of human history and of themselves which is spirit-filled but is neither denominational nor ideological. One graduate described her education as exposing her to "the inspiring, the enchanting and the inexplicable," providing a basis for her later interest in meditation and inner work. The experience of wholeness, of meaning and of self which their eduction has provided gives Waldorf graduates the possibility of both inner dialog and of co-creating with the spirit, or of working with "the secret order of the cosmos," to use Vaclav Havel's phrase.

There is yet another important dimension to Waldorf education which offers a healing perspective for the future. In *Education as a Social Problem*, Steiner remarks, "The great problem for the future will be a proper education. How will we be able to educate children so that they, as adults, can grow into the social, democratic and free areas of social life in a comprehensive way."[2] Here Steiner is referring to the principles of the threefold social order: of freedom in cultural life and education, equality in the political and rights life, and fraternity in economic life. He then suggests that a physical and social environment worthy of imitation in the ages from 0–7 provides the proper basis for the experience and understanding of freedom in adults, and that developing the right feeling for authority in the ages from 7–14 develops a proper basis for the life of rights among adults. "All education in this period of life will have to be consciously directed toward awakening in a child a pure, beautiful, feeling for authority; for what is to be implanted in him during these years is to form the foundation for what the adult is to experience in society as the equal rights of human beings."[3] He then added, during the same talk given in August of 1919, "Brotherhood, fraternity in economic life as it has to be worked for in the future, can only arise in human souls if education after the fifteenth year works consciously toward universal human love."[4]

What are we to make of these statements, what do they say about most forms of modern education, and how are we to understand them so that they can contribute to our human and social understanding?

If we ask whether family life and education today foster an environment worthy of imitation in the years from 0–7, respect for mature authority from 7–14, and a love of the truth and beauty of the human and natural world from 15 to 21, we would have to say no in many cases. The exposure to the media in the early years, the lack of respect for authority and the constant asking children what they want in the middle years of childhood, and the often instrumental and intellectual education in the high school years bode ill for the future of society if we accept the truth of Steiner's insights. To do so and to support them in education and family life means remembering the image of child and human development underlying Waldorf education. In the time from 0–7, the child is primarily engaged in building his or her physical instrument and everything in the surroundings—sounds, colors, words, moods, gestures—is taken in, imitated and becomes the basis of his/her physical health. The physical organism provides the foundation for the will of the adult human being. A healthy physical body and a well-developed will lead to experiencing and exercising freedom in oneself and in the world.

In the middle years of childhood, from 7–14, the etheric or life body of the child is developed. By watching children of this age carefully, we can note their interest and focus on fairness, rules and friendships, revealing their innate concern about right relationships. The experience of a wise authority, such as that of the class teacher or a parent, both helps to structure and form the life body of the child and instills a sense of equity and equality in the growing child which becomes the basis for a healthy feeling life in adulthood and for a healthy rights life in society.

The love of history, of learning and of the human enterprise built into the Waldorf high school curriculum fosters a sense of brotherhood and sisterhood in economic life in the adult, for in the years from

14–21, the astral or soul body of the young person is being developed. A love and appreciation for the world builds the understanding in the growing adolescent for our interconnection as part of the human community. It also forms the astral or soul body of the young person in a healthy way so that the needs of the human community can come to consciousness. This heart-based understanding leads to the recognition of our mutuality and the desire to serve the human community as opposed to exploiting it for personal gain.

If these deep spiritual and social insights of Rudolf Steiner about education are true, and my experience of Waldorf graduates suggests they are, then Waldorf education is truly an education for a better social future, for it fosters a healthy human being who in turn will create a more sustainable, peaceful and creative society. I believe it is this which has led me to spend much of my life supporting and working with Waldorf school communities. A good education is our best hope for a better society.

Endnotes

1. Douglas Sloan, "Imagination, Education, and Our Postmodern Possibilities," *ReVision: A Journal of Consciousness and Society*, Vol. 15, Number 2, Fall 1992, p. 51.
2. Rudolf Steiner, *Education as a Social Problem* (Steiner Press, Spring Valley, NY, 1969), p.12.
3. Ibid., p. 14.
4. Ibid., p. 16.

Acknowledgements

This book of essays has resulted from a great deal of collaborative work with Waldorf schools, with the many teachers, parents and administrative staff who have dedicated their lives to sustaining and developing Waldorf school communities in North America and around the world. It also was formed and enriched by many conversations with my students and colleagues in the Waldorf School Administration and Community Development Program at Sunbridge College in Spring Valley, New York. I am most grateful for the many insights shared during these mutual explorations and for the encouragement I received in elaborating the questions, thoughts and suggestions which find expression in these essays. The limitations of viewpoint and expression are mine, while the spirit of joint commitment to Waldorf education and to community building is ours.

I want to acknowledge the practical support which I received from Susan Dent and Lori Warner in turning often messily written notes and chapters into legible manuscript. I have also benefited from the many helpful comments and suggestions given by Paul Gierlach, Gary Lamb, Eric Utne and in particular Signe Schaefer, who has read many versions of these essays as they gradually took the form of this book. May our joint interest in the questions of building new educational communities give strength and encouragement to those carrying this work now and in the future.